THE THINGS THAT ARE NOT CAESAR'S

JACQUES MARITAIN
a thinker who has indelibly impressed the world of philosophy.

THE THINGS THAT ARE NOT CAESAR'S

JACQUES MARITAIN

A TRANSLATION OF
'PRIMAUTÉ DU SPIRITUEL'
MADE BY

J. F. SCANLAN

CHARLES SCRIBNER'S SONS
1931

PREFACE TO THE ENGLISH EDITION

This book was written on the occasion of a crisis which seriously divided the Catholics of France,[1] and which, if it has not entirely abated at the present day (for so long as a few of our brethren still refuse to listen to the voice of the Church, it will be impossible to say that all is well), has at any rate passed the acute stage. But, as I observed in the Preface to the French edition, what principally concerned me, my essential object, was to illustrate certain principles which I considered to be superior to time and circumstance and of universal validity, principles affecting the relations between the spiritual and the temporal which dominate the problems of culture and will always have for the philosopher a privileged interest.

A discerning reader, curious to discover the plan of composition of the book, would not be mistaken in supposing that the chapters into which it is divided correspond simply to the division of time into *past*, *present* and *future*, on the condition at any rate of understanding by *past*, the supra-temporal principles which protracted age-old controversies have induced the Christian mind to evolve and determine and which

[1] I have since published, in collaboration with a number of theologians and philosophers (MM. Lallement and Maquart, PP. Bernadot, Doncœur and Lajeunie), two books (*Pourquoi Rome a parlé* and *Clairvoyance de Rome*) explaining in greater detail the intrinsic reasons for the condemnation of the Action Française by Rome, which is to be considered primarily as a condemnation of *naturalism* in politics. *Cf.* more particularly the chapters, " Morale et Politique," and " Nature et Grâce," in *Clairvoyance de Rome*.

formerly took shape in historical forms that will never be seen again ; by *present*, a passing moment which, effectively present in 1927, has gone for good in 1930 ; by *future*, the new historical forms, the new problems, the new tasks, in accordance with which it may be presumed that these same unchanging principles will manifest themselves in the sphere of the changing.

This observation may be sufficient to dispose of certain criticisms, ineffectual because springing from a misconception, which are dictated by the notion prevalent in some minds that to evolve an intemporal substance of doctrine from a perishable past is to seek to eternalise that very past and to treat history as so much refuse. Professor Karl Winter [1] recently accused me, in a highly reputable Review of Public Law, of formulating archaic theses, adding also that the theology of laymen is always repudiated in the end by theology itself, because it attempts to settle quarrels that are not theological but sociological. Criticism of this kind is an unfailing source of joy and consolation to the author, considering that his object is precisely to break with pedantry. There is a sort of professional theology which is certainly not theology itself and which follows scientific fashions slavishly enough, as a rule after they have ceased to be fashionable ; affected with an incurable myopia which I will not call *historical* (for I am well aware that history is a precious instrument in the hands of a theologian, on condition that he makes use of it for thinking, not for dispensing himself from thinking), but which may be called *historicist*, such courageous *Fachtheologie*, I very well

[1] Ernst Karl Winter, of Vienna, *Kirche und Staat*, Kritische Bemerkungen zu Jacques Maritains Lehre von der *Potestas indirecta*, in *Zeitschrift für offentliches Recht*, Bd. IX, Heft I, 1 October, 1929.

realise, considers that the Church has now no other right than simply to station herself in sacristies, and deems it unseemly that recourse should be had to theological wisdom to enlighten us poor Christian laity, busy with the affairs of the world, on problems of culture and civilisation. This is precisely what the writer's feeling for intellectual hierarchies compels him, as a philosopher, to do.

I am, however, pleased to take advantage of the opportunity presented by this English edition to explain myself a little more fully, and to point out certain misconceptions which arise in the first place from the omission to distinguish between the possession of a power or a right (which depends on the essence of things) and the historical exercise of that power or right (which depends on circumstances and the progress of civilisations).

I am convinced that as regards the substance of their theological teaching on the relations between the spiritual and the temporal, between Church and State, the Popes of the Middle Ages and the Popes of modern times are agreed ; and it is precisely this common substance of doctrine which I have attempted to put before the modern reader. He will, however, do me the justice of believing that I am not so lacking in historical sense as not to realise that the circumstances of time and civilisation in which they both live have pretty well nothing in common. The Church, therefore, in our day, in her relations with States, acts according to modalities very different from those of the Middle Ages. The error in this case would be to think that, because the contingent modalities of practice vary, the doctrine determining the supreme spiritual standards of that same practice also similarly varies. To maintain that the rights which the Church claims for the spiritual power are merely a transitory expression and adaptation of particular juridical conceptions prevailing at different cultural epochs, in such a way, for example, that the Church, as M. Karl Winter thinks, would have invoked a " *direct power* " when Romanesque or Gothic was the fashion, an " *indirect power* " during the Baroque period, and in our day a merely *advisory and directive power* in regard to the temporal, is a facile opinion which for my own part—and I am no professional theologian—I consider as doing little credit to the stability of theological science,[1] and as absolutely devoid of any genuinely tested historical foundation. I hope to have shown in my book, summarily but yet convincingly enough, that, in their teaching as Popes, neither St. Gregory VII nor Boniface VIII ever claimed " *direct power* " over the temporal (this theory of the " direct power " is the invention of a few " extremist " theologians in the thirteenth and fourteenth centuries) ; that Bellarmine, the great exponent of the " *indirect power* "—recently raised by the Church to the rank of Doctor—intended only to express and in fact only did express the traditional doctrine of the Papacy ; and, finally, that if Leo XIII made no explicit reference to the " indirect power " (there is, nevertheless, a sufficiently obvious implicit allusion to it to be seen in a passage [2] in the encyclical *Immortale Dei*), he at any rate said nothing which

---

[1] The proposition that " *Ecclesia vis inferendae potestatem non habet neque potestatem ullam temporalem directam vel indirectam*," was, as is known, condemned by Pius IX. *Cf.* note 48.

[2] *Cf.* note 28.

was not in perfect harmony with that doctrine. It argues a very rudimentary logic and a most imperfect scientific method to exclaim immediately that there is a contradiction, without further consideration, when one is confronted with two texts (like the bull *Unam Sanctam* and the encyclical *Immortale Dei*), which, written in very different historical circumstances and illustrating different aspects of one same teaching, in reality merely complement one another with an interval of five centuries between. Anyone desirous of further information on this point may refer to the remarkable essay devoted to the " indirect power " by M. Charles Journet.[1]

It is this continuity of doctrine which I was concerned in the first place to establish and to emphasise, and the object of the chapter on " The Two Powers " was primarily doctrinal, its aim being to discover truths valid at all times. But the question of ascertaining whether the Church has by the nature of things a certain right of action over the temporal, and the question of ascertaining whether she makes use of such a right at particular epochs, and how, are two entirely different questions. The more important it seems to me to rise above time to return a proper answer to the former, the more important it seems to me to burrow deep down into time, and the mutability thereof, to return an answer to the latter. If evolutionists may be properly scandalised by the refusal to admit any but a homogeneous evolution by explicitation and increase in growth of (genuine) knowledge of the metaphysical or theological sort, disciples of the fixed-

---

[1] *La Pensée thomiste sur le pouvoir indirecte*, Vie Intellectuelle, 15th April, 1929. This paper will be separately published, with additions and some alterations, in the series *Questions disputées*.

type school may with equal propriety be scandalised by the admission of only a heterogeneous evolution for the contingent modalities of practice, or, if it be preferred, a series of revolutions due to the succession of opposite historical climates. The error in that case would be to think that, because the doctrine of the Church never varies or the supreme standards of her activity, the manner in which she adapts her activity to particular cases and continues to carry out in time the work of the Kingdom of God does not vary either.

So the public law of feudal times and the cultural conceptions then prevailing impressed their likeness upon the *exercise* made by the Church in the Middle Ages of her " indirect power " over the temporal : she had then a duty of maternal protection and education to discharge, of such capital importance, so far as Europe and the temporal kingdoms themselves were concerned, that *without ever adopting the doctrine of the " direct power,"* she made use of her " indirect power " in such a way as might sometimes *seem* to suggest such a doctrine ; nations had recourse naturally to her arbitration, and she was still to be seen towards the end of the fifteenth century dividing the world between two powers, imposing on each the duty of preaching the Gospel. At the time when the Christian States, having attained their majorities, immediately began to turn into despotisms, the " indirect power " of the Church was bound to act upon such States according to quite different modalities, juridically more precisely defined but practically less pliable and incapable of avoiding more irremediable collisions. In modern times, when the conception of the State has attained its full " laic " stature, the exercise of this same " indirect power " appears simply in the form of a counsel not proceeding so far as a formal order compelling obedience, in other words, in the shape of what some contemporary theologians and canonists call *potestas directiva* (an idea which is sufficiently clear so long as it is taken to refer to a modality of the practical activity, but is much less clear if it refers to a definite juridical entity [1]), and the use of it therefore tends to diminish considerably. In short, I think that, restricted to the modalities of practice, the thesis of a progressive transformation linked to the general evolution of civilisation has, in the reciprocal relations of the ecclesiastical and the temporal powers, the value of an evident fact, and I believe that it would not be difficult to come to an understanding with Fr. Bede Jarrett, O.P., on the interpretation to be given to the progress of history from this point of view.[2]

The Church never had recourse to the exercise of the " indirect power," even at the time of the struggle between the Empire and the Papacy, without feeling that she was wielding a dangerous weapon which ran the risk of giving umbrage to the irritable susceptibility of the temporal authority and letting loose a storm of angry passions, as was abundantly clear in the age of Philip the Fair, when that first king of modern times, with the help of his experts, I mean his lawyers, raised against her what would nowadays be described

[1] As M. l'Abbé Journet very pertinently observes (loc. cit., p. 666, note 1), the word *potestas* then becomes an improper description and ceases to mean a jurisdiction. " The régime of the *directive power*, strictly understood," writes Père de Groot, " appears to be far from consistent with the doctrine of the *Syllabus*, the decrees of the Popes, and the general teaching of the Doctors of the Church" (*Summa apologetica de Ecclesia Catholica*, 1906, p. 451).

[2] *Cf. A History of Europe*, esp. chaps. iv—viii (Sheed & Ward).

as a magnificently concerted press campaign. It was under the constraint of the necessity of the times, the social conditions of feudalism, and the fearful menace which the imperial despotism held over the liberty of the spiritual, that the Church was forced to have such energetic recourse in the Middle Ages to the exercise of such a right. I believe that in the new era into which we have entered since the final liquidation of the Holy Roman Empire, she will cease to exercise it otherwise than in the form of *counsels* or *directions*, which the nations will always expect from her supreme moral authority. It should be carefully defined that the " indirect power " is the right of intervention which the spiritual power possesses *over temporal things themselves* from the strict point of view of moral and spiritual interests, when superior interests of that kind happen to be involved in the temporal event. This power is not concerned in the least in the Action Française affair [1]—the Vatican has not ceased to say so in the most explicit fashion, and so much is plainly apparent from a consideration of the facts. The Pope condemned the Action Française, not because it constituted a certain political party, but because it imparted a certain teaching on the relations between politics, morals, and religion which he considered erroneous. The object of his intervention was *the prohibition of erroneous teaching threatening the integrity of the Catholic faith and morals and the rectitude of the Catholic mind* : there we are faced with *purely spiritual measures* directed in themselves, not against a temporal object in itself over which the Church has exercised a power of intervention from spiritual motives, but against an

[1] Or in the present Maltese crisis.

object itself spiritual—the teaching in question—coming in itself within the jurisdiction, the peculiar and exclusive jurisdiction, of the spiritual legislation.

That disturbances of the temporal sort may have followed in consequence of such a measure entirely spiritual in itself, that, for example, the political party of which M. Maurras is the leader may have been thereby put in a difficult position, is all very true, but, whereas in the exercise of the " indirect power " the measure taken by the legislator *of itself* affects the temporal, although indirectly, in the present case, on the contrary, the temporal is affected only *accidentally*, in a manner entirely extrinsic to the intention of the legislator and the very measure taken by him—in short, by a mere material repercussion. Deny this perfectly obvious distinction, upon the pretext that in both cases those who suffer the blow are affected in their temporal interests also, and you may as well immediately give up the faculty of thinking, for the distinction between the *per se* and the *per accidens* is the fundamental activity of that faculty ; you may as well say that, if the Church condemns a heretical doctrine, an action which has an inevitable repercussion on the sale of the books in which that doctrine is set forth, she is taking a measure which is not so much religious as commercial ; or that in proclaiming that there is only one God, an action which has an inevitable repercussion on the manufacture of, and trade in, idols, she is also performing not a religious but an economic act ; or that the moralist, in forbidding lying, intends to attack the national union of journalists ; or that the mathematician, in pondering over Zermelo's axiom, proposes to burn a certain quantity

xiii

of organic phosphorus in his cerebral matter. Here we are faced with connections involving the very structure of man and human life, and which the most purely spiritual decisions can set in motion. The case of the " indirect power," in which as a consequence of some such connection the Church considers herself entitled to act in the temporal itself *ratione peccati*, is merely a particular case, the most extreme and the most shocking to modern prejudice, of the much more general laws which concern both the mutual relations of the temporal and the spiritual and the inalienable liberty of the latter. It is because it is in my view sound tactics " to take the bull by the horns," and to grapple first with the clearest and most difficult case, that I began by establishing, in a first chapter, this theory of the " indirect power." All that then remained was to argue *a fortiori*. But the attentive examination of the facts which the writing of the book entailed had convinced me that the condemnation of the Action Française, in spite of my first impression, was in no way an exercise of the "indirect power." In addition, to avoid the slightest risk of ambiguity, I have refrained from mentioning again in subsequent chapters of the book the expression " indirect power." And that not only because in the particular case of the Action Française it was in fact a question of something utterly different, but also because in a general way I believe that as a matter of fact, in the period of history which we have just entered, the Church will refrain from intervening in the temporal and making use of her " indirect power " otherwise than in the form of a direction or counsel, as was said above.

Is there any foundation for such an opinion ? There

is in the first place one very remarkable positive fact, that Leo XIII, while making, as has been seen, an implicit allusion to the " indirect power " (he could hardly avoid doing so, for such a doctrine forms part of the common teaching of the Church), refrained from any specific reference to it in the documents of fundamental importance in which he deals with the Christian constitution of States. Pius X, Benedict XV and Pius XI, in dealing with the relations between Church and State, maintained the same reserve. Such silence is extremely significant, certainly not in regard to the impertinent hypothesis of some repudiation of doctrine, but in regard to the practical decision no longer to use in all its severity a right which has ceased to correspond to the conditions of the times. In the same order of ideas great attention ought to be paid to the notion of *Catholic action* on which H.H. Pius XI lays such vigorous stress. Such action is in itself essentially apostolic and supra-political : it is not unconcerned with things in the temporal and political order, but it affects them, not by a process of authority and jurisdiction, but by a vital and spiritual influence, animating from within and impregnating with Christian spirit the activities which concern them. I have certainly not waited for the criticisms of M. Karl Winter to make these observations.

Thereafter, and to come to intrinsic reasons, it is not simply enough to observe that the exercise of a power or right is useful only so far as it is consonant with the dispositions of the common conscience, which in the modern world is more and more jealous of the prerogatives and independence of the temporal authority : it is necessary to go very much farther. If it is true that in its progress through time culture passes under different constellations of dominant signs, it must be said that the *historical sky* or *historical ideal* under which a modern Christendom is conceivable is absolutely different from the historical sky or historical ideal of mediæval Christendom. The differences in question, which it would take too long to analyse here, seem to me to be grouped round one double central fact : round the ideological fact that the ideal or myth of " the realisation of liberty " has taken the place in modern minds of the ideal or myth of " force at the service of God "—and round the concrete fact that civilisation in the Middle Ages imperiously implied the unity of religion, whereas to-day it admits religious division.[1] It may so be realised that the peculiarities (and the deficiencies) of mediæval Christendom and those of the new Christendom, a *possibility* in modern times, are as it were in inverse relation to one another, linked in the one case to the dominance of the sign of force, in the other to that of the sign of liberty ; and it may also be realised at the same time that the primacy of Truth or the Church in civilisation, which could and ought to have been achieved under the sky of the Middle Ages by the rigorous exercise of all the rights of the spiritual power, must, on the contrary, be envisaged, under our historical sky, as a primacy of confidence and respect secured by the moral authority which a religiously divided world will come more and more to acknowledge—that is at any rate my hope—

[1] Some further observations on the problems affecting religion and culture will be found in my pamphlet, *Religion and Culture*, to be published by Messrs. Sheed & Ward as No. 1 of the series " Essays in Order," which I hope to develop and complete in a subsequent essay containing more concrete considerations.

in the Catholic Church " the teaching mistress and leader of all other societies," [1] and her visible head. That is the reason why I believe that, fully aware of the historical régime in which humanity is now engaged, the Church, whose dealings with men and history are as candid as the dealings of God, has decided with no *arrière-pensée* to give such a régime of civilisation a trial, and proposes henceforward to concern herself with nothing but a merely moral influence over the things of the temporal order.

Signor Mussolini, who has read *Primauté du Spirituel* (he did me the honour of quoting the book in one of his speeches), attempted one day to find an argument against the Catholic Church in the doctrine of the " indirect power," as though that doctrine caused the shadow of Gregory VII or Innocent III to hover over the anxious sovereignty of modern States. If some Protestant writer on other shores desired to imitate him with the object of provoking a religious controversy, I would answer him that such polemics are several centuries behind the time of history and the Church, and as far as this book is concerned are quite beside the question.

It is absurd for a writer to complain of being misunderstood, for such a misfortune is, as a general rule, his own fault : he needed only to explain his meaning more intelligently. It is not improper, however, to point out the awkward situation in which a philosopher is placed. Once he undertakes to evolve out of the long labour of speculation accomplished by his predecessors

---

[1] . . . *In eo dignitatis gradu statuitur Ecclesia in quo a suo ipsius Auctore collocata fuit, perfectae societatis, ceterarumque societatem magistrae* [not " *dominae* "] *ac ducis ;* . . . Pius XI, encyclical *Ubi arcano Dei* of the 23rd December, 1922.

b xvii

a supra-temporal substance of doctrine, and so to oppose something *eternal* to the errors of the present moment, it is believed that his intention is quite the reverse to oppose something of the *past* to the present, and to retrace his footsteps in time like Mr. Wells's machine. The individual then runs the risk of being singularly misunderstood and, for my own part, I conceive that I shall be branded for eternity with the character of *anti-modern*, the title given to one of my books in the secret desire to annoy my contemporaries.

I would here perform a great act of humility and invoke the authority of an *engineer* in support of the *philosophia perennis*. The activity of the technician is governed just as much by the same laws as govern human activity in general and may serve to illustrate the working of those laws in a more particularly striking way. I quote from the MS. used by F. W. Taylor as a basis for his lecture on " Success " [1] : " . . . Now for the *average* man no invention can be looked upon as a legitimate invention which is not an improvement on mechanism or processes or appliances which are already in existence, and which are successful. It is thoroughly illegitimate for the *average* man to start out to make a radically new machine, or method, or process, new from the bottom up, or to do things most of which have not already been done in the past. Legitimate invention should be always preceded by a complete study of the field to see what other people have already done. Then some one or more defects should be clearly recognised and analysed, and then it is entirely legitimate for the engineer to use his

[1] F. B. Copley : *Frederick W. Taylor*, vol. i, p. 77. Harper Bros. 1923.

ingenuity and his inventive faculty in remedying these defects, and in adding his remedy to the existing elements of the machine or the process which have already been found to work well. Any other invention than this should be looked upon as illegitimate, since it is almost sure to waste the money of your employer, as well as your own, and to result in partial, if not complete, disaster." If it be observed that in face of metaphysical realities, so lofty and so arduous that the jealousy of the gods, as Aristotle says, seems to deny us access to them, every man is an *average* man, the passage quoted will be considered a good and sound apology for philosophical work in the sense in which I understand it. Mr. Taylor begged his audience to look forward with their inventions, not backwards : that is the meaning of the motto—made famous by the great restorer of the Thomist philosophy, Pope Leo XIII—*vetera novis augere*.

To return to the object of this present work, I would have it observed once more that, if the misconceptions of certain critics have compelled me to insist in this preface upon the exact significance of the first chapter, it would not do to restrict the scope of the book to that chapter : the third chapter is, as a matter of fact, the most important.

It gives me pleasure that the book should be published in English through the kindness of Messrs. Sheed & Ward, and Mr. T. F. Burns, whom I take this opportunity of thanking ; it seems to me that every considered work upon the distinction between the spiritual and the temporal, between the things that are God's and the things that are Caesar's, is apt to dissipate prejudices fostered in certain minds by a deplorable ignorance

with regard to the Pope, as a " foreign sovereign."
The Pope is not a foreign sovereign : he is the visible
head of the mystical body, essentially supra-temporal,
supra-political, supra-national, supra-cultural, of which
Christ is the invisible head : he is, for the supreme
control of doctrine and the government of that Body,
the visibility, as it were, of Christ on this earth. His
kingdom is not of this world, and, if he does possess a
temporal sovereignty, it is as the minimum of body
required precisely to assure the full liberty of the
spiritual sovereignty peculiar to him ; if he is sovereign
of the Vatican City, it is precisely so that he shall be
neither Italian nor American, neither French nor
Chinese, so that he shall lose all human nationality, as
Christ was destitute of all human personality, to
belong exclusively to God.

September 1930.

PREFACE TO THE FRENCH EDITION

In presuming to discuss in this Essay questions simultaneously involving politics and religion, I would not have it thought that I have any intention of trespassing upon the domain of the teaching Church, for that would be absurd, or of abandoning the plane of philosophy for the contingencies of practical action, from which it is more than ever my desire to hold aloof. Certain essential principles, however, seem to have been lost sight of by many people, and it is of the first importance that they be recalled. I shall tell the truth or what appears to me such without regard for any other consideration. *Credidi, propter quod locutus sum.*

One single observation of our Lord is sufficient to settle everything and to denote the significance of the age we are about to enter. Seek first the kingdom of God and His justice and the rest shall be added unto you.

We do, however, need multiple explanations, and they must be based upon theology. We must, therefore, begin with an exposition of principles borrowed from that science.

Despite this forced loan from the theologians, the present Essay is still the work of a philosopher observing contemporary events from his own point of view. The crisis lately traversed by the Catholic members of the Action Française party and the decision taken by the Holy See in their regard are referred to at some length, but the problem discussed has a very much wider application. This book makes no claim to be an exhaustive study of that past crisis : it is concerned only with one aspect of it, which the author considers as of the greatest practical importance for the general interests of our culture and so, without failing in the respect due in that case to the purely doctrinal magistracy of the Church and her direct power over the spiritual, he has devoted his attention to the most acutely debated point in the whole conflict : the relation between the spiritual and the temporal, between doctrine and politics. Omitting or merely glancing at many useful considerations, we can the more easily rise to a point of view above particular cases and demonstrate certain essential principles concerning the present state of civilisation, the providential directions of the Church and the general primacy of the spiritual, principles which interest us above everything else.

The author would here take leave to adopt the last words of his master Thomas Aquinas. He hopes that he has written nothing offensive to divine Truth. Should he have done so, it was through ignorance, and he does not persist in his intention : should anything herein be ill-expressed, he leaves the whole to the correction of the Holy Roman Church.

25th May, 1927, *the Feast of St. Gregory VII.*

CONTENTS

CONTENTS

INTRODUCTION

Imperilled by a degraded civilisation which abandons man to the indetermination of matter, the mind must defend itself at all costs, assert its rights and its essential superiority. It is itself responsible for the evil. It attempted to hold truth captive, affected to disregard what surpasses the level of reason and, finally, reason itself. It is punished by the flesh for having sought to emancipate itself—by denying their existence—from the supreme realities which are to be assessed by the measure of God, not man. The control of the senses by reason and of reason itself by God is the essential condition of order and peace in the human being, and this can only be achieved through faith and supernatural love. The first subordination depends in practice upon the second. Adam shattered both : Christ re-established them by His grace and the gifts of His spirit. The error of the modern world and the modern mind consists in the claim to ensure the domination of nature by reason while at the same time refusing the domination of reason by supernature.

The scale of values has been thereby reversed ; the mind to-day is suffering the painful consequences— and the State as well. For the attribute " political animal " being, like the attribute " animal endowed with reason " whence it derives, essentially characteristic of the human being, the metaphysical history of man as a political animal—or society for that matter

—must necessarily follow the same course, with identical incidents of fortune, as the history of man as a rational animal—or the mind. The expulsion of the element of spirit and grace from intellectual and social life, that is to say, from what is specifically human, is the secret cause of the supremacy of matter which men find so burdensome and oppressive to-day.

This supremacy of matter must be resisted not only by the assertion of the rights of the mind and the reason but also by the asseveration of the supremacy of divine grace and the primacy of the spiritual.

Intermediary solutions now fade into the background. Man appears henceforth divided between the two extremes of the flesh and the spirit in the sense given to the phrase by St. Paul—a pure infra-human materialism and a divine super-human life ; the conflict would seem to be characteristic of the age into which humanity is about to enter. Reason must submit to the God which is spirit, if we are not to perish, and to the whole spiritual order established by Him. Our whole life must be orientated to that liberty of the spirit which is only to be obtained, through and in the truth, by the fullness of love.

It is in the " indirect power " of the Church of Christ over the temporal domain that the primacy of the spiritual finds its most concrete realisation in the most apparent, vivid and significant manner. The first chapter is devoted to a consideration of this question.

A second chapter examines from the point of view of this same primacy the crisis lately traversed by a number of Catholics in France.

An attempt has been made in the third chapter to ascertain some of the main lines of conduct suggested to our reflection and for our action, in the present state of the world, by the principle of the primacy of the spiritual considered in all its extent.

I

THE TWO POWERS

1. THE SPIRITUAL POWER AND THE TEMPORAL POWER

1. NOTHING is more important for the freedom of souls and the good of mankind than properly to distinguish between these two powers : nothing, in the language of the day, has so great a *cultural* value. It is common knowledge that the distinction is the achievement of the Christian centuries and their glory.

The pagan City, which claimed to be the absolute *whole* of the human being, absorbed the spiritual in the temporal power and at the same time apotheosised the State. Its ultimate worship of the Emperors was the sure consequence of an infallible internal logic. "Even the Christian Emperors and Constantine, the first of them, did not immediately repudiate certain symbols of divine honour, such as the building of temples and the celebration of games in their honour. The iconoclasts destroyed the images of Christ and the Saints at Byzantium, but respected the images of the Emperor. It was not until the fourth century that the Emperor Gratian gave up using the title of *Pontifex Maximus*. And to avoid running down the whole subsequent course of history, it will be sufficient to observe that by the blasphemous beast ' come up out of the sea ' and the other beast ' come up out of the earth,' ' that did great signs,' both

B   I

securing the adoration denied to the Lamb, the Apocalypse intends to symbolise the profaning and usurping civilisation of all times and all countries " [1].[1]

The Lord Christ said : *Render therefore to Caesar the things that are Caesar's : and to God, the things that are God's.* He thereby distinguished the two powers and so doing emancipated the souls of men.

2. Every act of ours may, according to different formal aspects, be referred at one and the same time to the particular good of ourselves or our neighbour as an individual, to the common good of the family or the State and to the transcendent common good of the whole universe, that is to say, to God Himself. Hence three hierarchised ordinations concerning respectively the " monastic " in Aristotle's phrase or private ethics, the " economic "[2] or politics, both branches of social ethics—and morals or general ethics dominating and enveloping the whole [2].

The State being the most perfect natural community (that is to say, the most capable of being self-sufficient) which mankind can form in this world, it is of supreme importance to draw the distinction and define the relations of subordination between politics, which are ordered to the whole of the terrestrial State as to their proximate and specific end, and ethics which are ordered to the divine transcendent whole. The subordination of politics to · ethics is absolute and even infinite, being based on the subordination of ends ; for the good of the State is not God Himself, and remains far, far inferior to the

[1] The figures refer to the notes at the end of the book.

[2] In the Aristotelian sense of the science of the good conduct of the family or domestic society.

supreme beatitude of man. " The subordination is such—it is indeed infinite—that the strongest expressions employed to indicate it will always be exceeded by the reality. The Ancients, even Aristotle himself, did not fully realise it [3], because they did not perceive with sufficient clarity that the supreme good of human life is God Himself. Christianity was needed to make that fully clear ; and when the gift of understanding, whose specific function it is, shows the Christian that everything which is not God is annihilated before God—*quidquid Deus non est nihil est, et pro nihilo computari debet* [4]—it shows him also that the end of politics is nothing in comparison with the end of ethics " [5].

The Ancients were no more successful in emancipating the free act from the ties which bind it to *this world*. Christianity was needed for the full realisation that the free act, considered purely in its freedom and in the secret node wherein the moral universe is born, is bound by no tie to the world or consequently to the State which is parcel of the world, but solely to God, the primary free agent, and the created will, the second free agent ; so that the secrets of the heart by their very nature escape the natural glance of the angels, and yet to the angels the whole spectacle of this world is due [6]. Neither the Prince of this world nor any prince of the nations can know anything of the spiritual heaven concealed in the recesses of our being and containing the kingdom of God, *regnum Dei intra vos est* : Christ alone can penetrate it by His priestcraft —and after Him, by the Sacrament of Penance which entitles them to know such secrets, the priests of the New Law, covered with the Blood of Christ.

3

Although *formally considered as part of the State*, every act of his can be referred to the common good of the State,[1] man, *considered in the absolutely peculiar and incommunicable quality of his liberty and as ordered directly to God as to his eternal end*, himself enjoying therefore the dignity of a whole (to a more eminent degree than the entire physical universe, because God is much more intimately the end of a soul than of the whole universe of bodies), under this formal aspect escapes inclusion in the political ordination : *Homo non ordinatur ad communitatem politicam secundum se totum et secundum omnia sua.*[2]

3. But in that order of eternal life the individual is no more self-sufficient—even less—than in the temporal. By the very fact of being ordered to the beatific vision, he is parcel of a superior whole, of a State which is a much more perfect unit than the terrestrial State (inasmuch as it is one single mysterious body living with the supernatural life which it receives from Christ), and to which every member is much more closely bound than he is to the terrestrial State, for we need the terrestrial State for the normal development of our nature, not for participation in the essence of humanity itself, whereas none can be made to share, through sanctifying grace, in the divine nature without belonging either visibly or invisibly (*sive re sive voto*) to the Church ; the angels are members of it no less than men [7], and when we have finally become gods by vision—*ego dixi : dii estis*—we belong to it more than ever, because it is essential for it to make us

[1] St. Thomas Aquinas, *Sum. Theol.*, ii–ii, 58, 5.
[2] *Ibid.*, i–ii, 21, 4, ad 3.

4

enter the company, through the life of grace, of the Blessed Trinity Itself. That State is truly divine, but no less truly human, and therefore visible, the continuation of the Incarnation in our midst—parts of it have been impressed in baptism on this earth with the seal of effective incorporation and all men are created for incorporation in it—its invisible head is Jesus Christ, its visible head he who was charged by Christ to feed His sheep ; it is in the world—without being of the world and because it is not of the world—the seat of the spiritual power which directs it towards its end and of which the Pope, as Vicar of God, is the supreme depository.

Each of us, therefore, belongs to two States—a terrestrial State whose end is the common temporal good, and the universal State of the Church whose end is eternal life. " There are two peoples in one same enclosure, one same human multitude, and these two peoples give occasion for two distinct lives, two principates and a dual juridical system " [8]. Towards the end of the fifth century, Pope Gelasius wrote that " there are two things by which this world is chiefly governed : the sacred authority of the pontiffs and the power of kings " [9]. In the nineteenth century Leo XIII said likewise : " God has divided between the ecclesiastical and the civil power the task of procuring the well-being of the human race. He has appointed the former to divine, the latter to human things. Each of them is supreme in its own sphere (*utraque potestas est, in genere suo, maxima*) ; each is enclosed within perfectly defined boundaries, delimited in exact conformity with its nature and principle. Each is therefore circumscribed within a sphere in

5

which it can act and move in virtue of its own peculiar laws " [10].

It is only too clear, however, that these two distinct powers are not on the same plane. One is above the other. The terrestrial State, being a moral whole, as such owes duties to God [11]. In its own sphere it is subject to the universal *temporal* sovereignty of Christ [12] ; for Christ, as Man, received from God dominion " over the works of His hands " and " all things have been subjected under His feet," [1] and it is from Him that kings and the heads of States and every human power derive their authority ; the State, as such, is bound to observe His Law and the precepts of His morality. As a moral and religious agent, it is, therefore, itself part of the Church. " The Emperor is in the Church, not above it," said St. Ambrose [13]. The State, therefore, is indeed sovereign in its own domain, but its domain is subordinate, so that its sovereignty can be neither absolute nor universal. There is only one universal absolute sovereignty, the sovereignty of the Creator. The sovereignty of the Church, universal through the whole range of salvation, is clearly more extensive and elevated than that of the State. To distinguish between the temporal and the spiritual is simultaneously to affirm the subordination of the former to the latter. Do not the divine words which are the root of the distinction indicate also the subordination ? Render, therefore, to Caesar the things that are Caesar's, and to God the things that are God's : were the things that are Caesar's not God's things before they became Caesar's ? [14].

[1] St. Paul, Hebrews ii. 8.

II. THE SPIRITUAL SOVEREIGNTY OF CHRIST AND THE CHURCH AND THE INDIRECT POWER

4. The universal kingship of Christ has a dual nature : it is both spiritual and temporal. But it is "above all spiritual and mainly concerned with spiritual things." [1] It is this *spiritual* kingship of Christ, founded upon His *capital grace* [15], which here calls for consideration. In that sphere Christ is not only the interior principle of our supernatural life—the special province, as has been observed, of His priesthood [16]—unceasingly communicating to us the grace earned by His Passion which God also infuses into us by the conjoined instrument of His humanity, the most holy movements of His mind and heart ; He possesses also a supreme power of government over the whole spiritual domain, the special province of His kingship, in virtue of which He leads His people of souls to eternal life, enacts laws, pronounces judgements, sees to the carrying out of His orders, establishes His kingdom by triumphing over sin and death. He is the head of the Body of the Church. "The head," says St. Thomas, "exercises a double influence over the limbs ; an interior influence, for the head transmits the power of movement and sensation to the limbs, and an influence of exterior government, for the head directs man in his exterior acts by the sight and the other senses of which it is the seat." [2]

To these two influences the dual power of order and jurisdiction transmitted to the Church may be related [17] : the former, involving the economy of the sacra-

---

[1] Pius XI, Encyclical *Quas Primas*.
[2] St. Thomas Aquinas, *Sum. Theol.*, iii, 8, 6.

ments, being in the first place a participation in the priesthood of Christ (men are here mere instruments, for " the interior influence of grace can proceed from Christ alone Whose humanity, combined with divinity, possesses the virtue of justifying ") [1] ; the latter, involving the direction of the mystic Body by the teaching of doctrine and laws, being a communication of His spiritual kingship (men are here responsible, albeit subordinate agents, for " the influence which Christ exercises through His exterior government can be communicated to others : these others are the heads of the Church . . . they are heads because they take the place of Christ ").[2]

So " in the person of Peter, the other apostles and their successors, the Church received directly from God, through our Lord Jesus Christ, the task of leading souls, by the light of revealed dogma and Christian morals, to eternal life. Her power corresponds to her divine mission and embraces all who have received the character given in baptism and everything necessary or useful to lead them to their last end.

" *In spiritual things, such power is direct.* Spiritual things are the province of faith and morals, of salvation, in which the Church exercises her infallible magistracy by teaching the supernatural and natural truths of faith, the precepts and counsels contained in the deposit of divine revelation of which she is the custodian.

" It is her function on that score to interpret the teaching of revelation with regard to the use of material things, to say what things should be rendered to

[1] St. Thomas Aquinas, *Sum. Theol.*, iii, 8, 6.
[2] *Ibid.*

Caesar and what are owing to God. This direct power is also clearly responsible for the administration of the sacraments, which are the channels of grace, the religious discipline not only of clerks but also of laymen considered as of the faithful, the regulation of theological studies, religious instruction in schools and everything which bears a sacred character or is necessary to divine worship, such as churches in which the Holy Sacrifice is offered. . . .

" The consequence is that the Church has an *indirect power* over *temporal things* " [18].

5. What is so described [1] is the power possessed by the Church over the temporal not as such, but *as affecting the spiritual order of salvation*—not because of the temporal good itself to be procured but rather with a view to *the denunciation or avoidance of sin, the preservation of the good of souls and the maintenance of the liberty of the Church*. Here it is not a question, as in the theory of the direct power over the temporal maintained by certain theologians in the Middle Ages,[2] of a power distinct from the spiritual power, it is the spiritual power itself, the spiritual sword drawn against the things of the world because of the eternal interests at stake. And that sword is not kept in the sheath.

In Christ, this power of intervening in the temporal with a view not to the temporal itself, but to the spiritual, " is part and parcel of the spiritual kingship,

---

[1] The expression *indirect* power is open to misconception. It might lead to the belief that the right in question affects the temporal only by way of repercussion from the measures taken with regard to the spiritual. This is not so. This right directly affects the temporal itself, but only *because of* the spiritual.

[2] Cf. Appendix I.

for it is at its service and, in a manner of speaking, its instrument. *Ubi est unum propter alterum*, Aristotle had already observed, *ibi tantum unum esse videtur*.

"And the older theologians were justified in describing such a power as instrumental. *Christus secundum quod homo*, writes Bannez, *habuit instrumentalem potestatem dominii universalis circa omnia temporalia.*" [1]

In the Church of Christ such a power is a participation in the spiritual kingship of Christ. Peter has it for the simple reason that Christ transmitted it to him as His representative on earth with the keys of the kingdom of Heaven. "What is the Church?" asked Bossuet. "The Church is Jesus Christ, but Jesus Christ diffused and communicated" [19].

Because the *indirect* power over the temporal is merely the spiritual power itself applied to temporal things on account of the spiritual interests involved, the principles governing the acts properly so called of the indirect power are also applicable and *a fortiori* valid in the reactions which measures taken in virtue of the *direct* power (doctrinal or disciplinary) over the spiritual may, in certain cases, have in the temporal sphere.

We will therefore attempt to establish in the first place the doctrine of the indirect power, the prototype for reference in such questions, it being well understood that the same doctrine is also applicable, and with stronger reasons, to such reactions as the temporal may suffer from measures in themselves exclusively spiritual. The same problem is involved, of the

[1] Cf. C. V. Héris, *Revue des sciences phil. et théol.*, July 1926. This instrumental power proceeds from the *spiritual* kingship of Christ and is quite a different thing from His *temporal* kingship.

general subordination of human things to the divine things of which the Church is the custodian.

The terrestrial State is itself compelled by an inner necessity to postulate such a superior right in the City of God. It is in fact ordered to a temporal common good which is not of a material kind only, but also and mainly moral : the humanly good life (the virtuous life) [20] of the multitude assembled in a social body, *communicatio in bene vivendo* [21]. Now an upright moral life in this world assumes that man is ordered to his last end, a supernatural end attainable only through Christ ; the good of the State must, therefore, be ordered to that same supernatural last end which is the end of every individual man ; civil society must pursue the common temporal end so far as it enables man to obtain eternal life [22] ; politics themselves, to be what they ought, insist that the spiritual be predominant, that the order with eternal salvation for its object predominate over the order designed to secure merely the good things of this world ; the State is not truly served if God is not served first. The rule of conduct governing individual and social life being unable to dispense with the supernatural order, and complete political wisdom, strictly speaking, depending on theology,[1] the Prince, if he is to perform his functions properly, must himself be learned in that science and take counsel from those who have charge of it. So St. Louis consulted St. Thomas. "The King," wrote the latter, "ought to procure the good life for the multitude in this world so far as it is likely to secure beatitude in Heaven ; he must therefore prescribe the things which conduce to such happiness and as far

[1] Cf. Appendix II.

11

as possible proscribe their opposites. And the way to true beatitude and the obstacles thereto are known by the divine law, the teaching of which is the province of the priestly ministry " [23].

The order of agents, however, corresponds to the order of ends. If the end of the terrestrial government is subordinate to the end of the spiritual government, the latter must have power over the former, must be able to direct it by its counsel and, if the interest of souls so require, control it by its orders [24].

The Church has thus a right of authority over the political or the temporal itself, not because of political things, but because of the spiritual principle involved. *One sword is under the other :* not to be oppressed in its own sphere, but to be controlled and directed by the upper sword as regards the latter's own sphere. The special interventions of the spiritual in temporal matters are motivated by one object only, the avoidance or repression of sin. " Let nobody therefore imagine," wrote Innocent III to the bishops of France in 1204, " that We claim to meddle with or seek to diminish the jurisdiction of the illustrious king of the Franks any more than he desires or ought to hinder Ours. . . . We do not claim to judge of the fee, for the judgement thereof is his province . . . but to sit in judgement upon sin, which We are undoubtedly entitled to censure. We have the power, and it is also Our duty, to visit Our censure on any person whomsoever. . . . *Non enim intendimus judicare de feudo, sed decernere de peccato* " [25]. Similarly it is the *ratio peccati* which is alleged by Innocent IV against Frederick II and by Boniface VIII against Philip the Fair ; the *ratio peccati* is the essential justification for the interventions of the Church in temporal affairs.

6. This doctrine is unchangeable. It may have been presented under different aspects : it has not altered in essentials throughout the centuries. What was described in the Middle Ages as the doctrine of the two swords—at all events in the sense in which it was understood by St. Bernard and St. Thomas Aquinas [1] as in pontifical documents—is essentially identical with what has been described since Bellarmine [26] and Suarez [27] as the doctrine of the indirect power— at all events if the latter be taken without attenuation. Anyone paying sufficient attention to the substance of things underlying the various incidents of history will perceive that one same teaching is imparted by Boniface VIII in the Bull *Unam Sanctam* and by Leo XIII in the Encyclical *Immortale Dei* ; and for a complete idea of the indirect power, both these great documents should be simultaneously borne in mind.

There are in effect two complementary aspects in the doctrine of the indirect power. On the one hand it assumes the distinction of the two powers and the sovereignty of the civil power in its own sphere ; Leo XIII lays special stress upon it, but is still careful to point out that the authority of the Church extends to temporal things only so far as they come into relation with whatever affects the salvation of souls and the worship of God [28]. Moreover, as the Church makes a special intervention on that score only in a case where the things of civil sovereignty happen to affect the peculiar object of the

[1] Cf. Appendix III.

13

sacred sphere in some particular way, the result is that so long as its subordinate but autonomous province affects the good of souls only to the very general extent to which the existence of a temporal order may usefully serve that good, civil sovereignty is free to attend to its own business without having to obey [29]. On the other hand, this same doctrine of the indirect power asserts the general subordination of the temporal to the spiritual and consequently the right of the spiritual power to impose restrictions, wherever necessary because of some connection with the good of souls, on the sovereignty of the civil power. Boniface VIII lays special stress upon it : " *Oportet autem gladium esse sub gladio et temporalem auctoritatem spirituali subjici potestati* " [30], but is still careful to point out that the temporal sovereignty remains none the less real [31]. It is one of the most pernicious of modern illusions to think that there can be no sovereignty, liberty or independence which is not *absolute*. If such were the case, no man would be free or a king unless he were God.

To demonstrate this subordination of the temporal to the spiritual, which he compares to the subordination of the body to the soul [32], St. Thomas, as we have seen, bases himself on the subordination of ends [33], which requires that the authority which impels towards the ultimate end shall be able to control by its teaching or counsel or, if need be, by its orders, authorities which impel towards the intermediate end, and that kings be subject to the Supreme Pontiff under the law of Christ. It should be carefully observed that from this point of view the indirect power is considered in a very universal way as including not only particular interventions of the Church by counsel or express orders *ratione peccati*, but also the governing influence she exercises over temporal things by her general teaching and the *education* she gives the nations. A temporal sovereignty so *formed* in spirit, a truly Christian state, would proceed of its own accord to Christian ends and the special interventions of the Church, whose maternal care unceasingly envelops the nations, would be merely additional to such a spontaneous movement for the purpose of completing and perfecting it. So, in normal conditions of civilisation, that is to say, if nations and governments were what they ought to be, the indirect power would find as it were its natural expression simply in their instinctive docility to the law of the Gospel and the general teaching of the Church and also, when the Church thought fit, to her counsel in any particular case. It is true that men are rarely what they ought to be, and coercive measures, however exceptional, are in fact sometimes necessary. The indirect power then extends as far as the primacy of the spiritual requires ; for the Church is not disarmed, her right is effective and efficient.

Such a right is not confined merely to the spiritual in the temporal : because of the spiritual and its relation to the temporal, it embraces also the temporal itself, it can quash and annul laws promulgated by a State, it can extend to deposing kings and emperors, if the danger to which they expose souls is too great, and set their subjects free from their oath of allegiance. For " a man can lose his right of sovereignty," says St. Thomas [34], " by decree of justice as much for a crime against the Faith as for any other fault. . . .

A baptised Sovereign, who abjures the Faith, runs the risk of causing a great corruption of the Faith among his subjects. . . . Once he is excommunicated by decree of justice for having broken with the Faith, his subjects are freed from his sovereignty and their oath of allegiance " [35]. To be surprised that this should be the case, a man must have lost the sense of reality and live only among appearances and words. The Church could cease to assert her right only if she ceased to be conscious of the divine good which it is her mission to dispense to mankind. We should be grateful to St. Gregory VII, to Innocent III, to Gregory IX, to Boniface VIII, for having given this unhappy world the strongest testimony of the rights and power of the Spirit. Canossa will always remain the consolation of free minds. " We fear no threats," said St. Thomas à Becket, the legate of Pope Alexander III, to Henry II of England, " because the Court from which we come is accustomed to give orders to emperors and kings " [36].

Whatever the fashionable theological opinions of the time may have been, it is the power of the spiritual sword applied *as such* to political affairs, in other words the " indirect power over the temporal," which is the foundation and explanation of the authoritative acts of those great Popes with regard to emperors and kings [37]. Their intervention was determined according as it was required by the rights of God, the liberty of the Church and the salvation of souls [38]. It was in virtue of the indirect power that St. Gregory VII asked : " Can any man doubt that the priests of Christ are as the fathers and tutors of kings and princes and all the faithful ? " [39]—and Innocent III

16

declared : " It was His will that We should sit above princes and pass judgement upon them " [40]. Feudal law and mediæval public law merely provided the indirect power with certain means—suitable to a given historical state [41] and to the needs of terribly troubled times—of being exercised for the salvation of Christian civilisation. If the methods of applying such a power vary in the course of the ages, it remains in substance unchanged and persists in the hands of the Church as an absolutely normal right, required by the very nature of things, a right the exercise of which could cease only if God abandoned the world to itself, that is to say to perdition.

Formerly, when the political régime of the nations involved heads which were truly sovereign, it was above all they who were as a general rule affected by the indirect power [42]. At the present day it is not unusual for it to affect even simple citizens or groups of citizens. Pius X placed this beyond doubt in condemning as modernist the following propositions : " Every Catholic, because he is at the same time a citizen, has the right and the duty, disregarding the authority of the Church and heedless of her wishes, counsel and demands, in defiance even of her rebukes, to pursue the public good in any way he thinks best. To prescribe a line of conduct for the citizen on any pretext whatever is an abuse of the ecclesiastical power which it is a duty to resist with all one's strength." [1]

7. It makes a Frenchman blush to think that Gallican governments long compelled [43] the epis-

---

[1] Encyclical *Pascendi*, Denzinger-Bannwart's Enchiridion Symbolorum, etc., 2092. The references throughout are to the 16th and 17th edition, Freiburg, 1928.

copate to suppress the lessons in the breviary relating to St. Gregory VII, because that Pope deposed the Emperor Henry IV. Strictly speaking, to refuse the spiritual power the right to intervene in politics is to deny the existence of an independent spiritual power. It is, in fact, to assert that moral values affecting political acts depend upon the temporal power alone and so to transfer to the temporal power *pro tanto* jurisdiction over things spiritual [44]. As often as the temporal refuses the spiritual its right over the temporal, the temporal *pro tanto* encroaches upon the spiritual. "The king," wrote Fénelon in his notes, "is in practice more head of the Church than the Pope in France. *Liberties vis-à-vis the Pope, servitude vis-à-vis the King*" [45]. Three centuries earlier, the apologists of Philip the Fair, on the pretext of asserting the independence of the State and the patriotic obligations of the Church, "in reality clamoured for the subjection of the Church to the State and the right of the State to use, control, and regulate the moral and social force represented by the Church. The ultimate end they pursued was the public and national interest which, they contended, it was the function of the State alone to administer with a despotism beyond the reach of any law" [46]. Again, considering the matter the other way round, there is no spiritual act but translates itself in some way, either by itself or its more or less remote consequences, into the exterior and temporal order, so that driven to the extreme, the absolute autonomy of the temporal would end by subjecting—through the temporal aspect which human acts affect—the whole of the spiritual to the temporal. For this reason the pretext of such autonomy may suffice to give an appearance of legality to the most savage persecutions. The regalian formula " complete independence of the temporal " reeks of deceit and death, like the formula of the " inviolability of the lay laws " which has succeeded it at the present day.

That unwarrantable " clerical interferences " may occur in the temporal sphere nobody would be so foolish as to deny. *Malum ut in pluribus in specie humana* is a statistical law as true of the clergy as of the laity, and every man entrusted with any power over other men may be tempted to abuse it. But it is a humiliating thing for the intellect and essentially pernicious to deny a right in order to get rid of a practical inconvenience. On the other hand, the fact is that such interferences are in most cases made not by superiors acting within the limits of their functions, still less by the Church herself acting in the person of the Supreme Pontiff, but by ecclesiastics exceeding the limits of their legitimate authority. *Nemo militans Deo implicat se negotiis saecularibus* [1] ; it is devoutly to be wished that the clergy refrain from the business of the world, that priests abstain from politics in their parishes, that bishops concern themselves little with changes of government, that the laity be spared the spectacle of priests and religious consumed with a burning passion for a party—democratic, nationalist or racial—and adopting its prejudices and hatreds. Such contaminations of the spiritual by the temporal have nothing in common with the right of the spiritual over the temporal for the avoidance of sin and are even quite the reverse.

[1] St. Paul, 2 Timothy ii. 4.

Let it be added that the abuses mentioned seem as a general rule to have been most prevalent where the power of the Pope was weakest and regalian principles most vigorous : in the time of the concordats more than in the Middle Ages. And the reason is not far to seek, because they proceed in the first place from a sort of particularism which yokes the authority of religion to the service of certain social groups or certain human interests. It is in the universality of the Church and divine interests that the remedy for this evil is to be found. The power of the Pope is the strongest guarantee the nations can have against it. By the very fact of his being vigilant in the sphere of politics itself to protect the interests of the spiritual, he is also their strongest bulwark against every other abuse : " The truth is that in anything salutary to the general good in a State, in anything useful to protect the people against the licence of princes careless of its good, in anything which might prevent the unjust encroachments of the State on the commons or the family, in anything involving honour, human personality and the maintenance of the equality before the law of every citizen, the Catholic Church has ever taken the initiative, bestowed her patronage on all such things and conferred upon them her protection." . . .[1]

It is instructive to consider the pride of States and mortal kings persistent in their determination throughout four centuries to reject the tutelage of the spiritual power [47] and to claim an *absolute* sovereignty, only to end by fatal necessity (it is not matter which holds States together but the spirit) in revolutionary and

[1] Leo XIII, Encyclical *Immortale Dei*.

democratic crises and in our day in the largest diminu-
tions of sovereignty from below—I mean by the very
development and tyranny of the economic, the law of
material " progress " making modern States less and
less capable of being self-sufficient units, less and less
of a " perfect society," at a time when their national
particularism in the moral order is carried to the
furthest extreme.

Be the claims of sovereigns and nations as they may,
the Church, for her part, has not ceased to proclaim
her imprescriptible right to intervene in temporal
matters *ratione peccati*. This is not a mere opinion, but a
" theologically certain " truth, formally taught by the
doctrinal magistracy of the Church [48].

III. THE EXTENT OF THE INDIRECT POWER

8. The *formal object* of the indirect power is perfectly
delimited : it is the *ratio peccati*, the moral element
affecting the spiritual good and the life of the Church
which happens to be involved in the temporal. The
subject matter of the power is everything in exterior and
temporal things which may admit of that formal
reason, in other words has a moral value, concerns the
moral activity of the human being [49]. This is
practically unlimited : any temporal arrangement,
any kind of temporal activity may, if the *ratio peccati* is
sufficiently seriously implicated, necessitate the exercise
of the indirect power.

There are in the concrete no morally indifferent
human acts. Some acts, considered in themselves
and from the point of view of the object, are doubtless
neither good nor bad : but nobody performs them

unless for a given end and in certain given circumstances. They are on that account then good or bad in fact, have necessarily a moral value [50]. Therefore as each of us is citizen of two States, the terrestrial State and the City of God, so each of our acts is a point liable to be affected by an at all events potential relation to the common good of the terrestrial State and a relation to the common spiritual good of the City of the Saints, the supreme and sovereign custodian of moral values. If an act, in itself of an individual or domestic kind, affects in a sufficiently important way the good of the terrestrial State, the legislator may subject it to the dispositions of the civil law. So also if an act, in itself of a temporal kind, affects in a sufficiently serious way the good of the City of God—no longer a temporal, but a spiritual good—the spiritual power may subject it to its ordinances.

When it so intervenes in regard to things dependent in themselves on the civil authority or the activity of the citizen, it may then be said to intervene in temporal matters " connected with " the general good of souls [51]. It must be thoroughly realised here that the relation to the common good of the Church may depend not only on the nature of the object, but also on the contingent historic conditions, the ends pursued and the circumstances involved. Things which are not bad of their kind may so become accidentally vitiated and thereby constitute a danger to souls ; consider, for example, kingship falling into the hands of a heretic or pervert or the activity of the partisans of some political ideal which, although lawful in itself, may tend to make them lose sight of truth or detach them from the order of charity. Any sort of temporal

22

work—not only a public decree or legislative enact-
ment [52], the raising of taxes, the declaration of war
or a treaty of peace, but also the activity of a professional
or syndical or political group, the exercise of some
particular civic right [53]—may come into special
connection with the good of souls, once it becomes for
instance the occasion of some spiritual aberration or
happens to affect sufficiently seriously the rights and
liberty of the Church or the orientation of the faithful
towards eternal salvation.

9. Who is to be the judge of such a connection and
the gravity of the spiritual interests involved ? Clearly
the Church alone. " The Church must judge not
simply according to the laws of her jurisprudence, but
first and foremost, let it be carefully observed, according to what is required of her maternal responsibility,
which is limitless. . . . Every instinct of the Christian
reason, so far from tending to confuse the two powers,
human and divine, rather inclines to make no distinction between the maternal office of the Church and her
suzerainty, to make one the foundation and the measure
of the other, to stop the Church's right of intervention
only at limits imposed by herself, to acknowledge
her character of arbiter and counseller, not only
beneficent but also necessary, and, let it be said,
sovereign and unlimited in practice.

" For the Christian relates the public sovereign
right of the Church to the four inviolable prerogatives
which attest her divine origin and constitution.
Unity necessarily gathers round her and brings within
her fold all nations and states. Sanctity preserves
her from both the errors and the assaults of man-made

laws. Catholicity exempts her from every national servitude. Apostolicity is the seal of her priesthood and the bulwark of her jurisdiction. These divine guarantees have an element, if not of the specifically infinite, at any rate of the unlimited in their application " [54]. And it is for the Church alone, for the Pope alone to determine, *hic et nunc*, in every particular case, the extent of such application : to judge on what occasions and in what circumstances what temporal matter calls for the exercise of the indirect power on the ground of its relation to the life of souls and their last supernatural end. For " only the teaching Church is qualified to judge of the *relation* between temporal things and the last supernatural end to which it is her duty to lead us " [55]. Here we stand at the parting of the ways where every human conception of the Church, however elevated, proves inadequate. I can understand that so extensive a power should scandalise unbelievers and heretics. But it is not necessary, it would even be absurd for those who do not and those who do know what the Church is to form the same idea of what her rights are. That Catholics should be scandalised or disquieted is what is abnormal and disquieting.

Moreover, if we consider things in their proper proportions in time, we shall perceive, as Joseph de Maistre observed, that the Popes have very rarely used the formidable sanctions given them by the indirect power. What earthly power, possessing such a right, would use it as a rule with such moderation ? The Church is not anxious to put our strength of soul to the test ; she knows that perpetual worrying is always a danger even to governments : she exercises her authority in temporal matters only in cases of urgent necessity—which also shows that all the more importance is to be attached to such interventions.

I would add that it is for the prudence of the Church alone to determine, according to circumstances and the gravity of every particular case, the weight of importance her intervention should assume in the very rich and subtle scale which ranges from a mere request or suggestion or recommendation to a formal order and the most definitive juridical proceedings : in modern terminology, to give the exercise of her indirect power a *directive* or *imperative* character, the value of a mere counsel or a positive command.

IV. CHRISTIAN OBEDIENCE

10. The virtue of obedience is an exalted virtue, eminently reasonable ; it is not in the least servile or blind, but requires on the contrary the greatest freedom of spirit and the strongest discernment. If a superior, even a lawful superior, exceeds the limits of his jurisdiction or gives an order opposed to the command of a more exalted superior, he need not be obeyed. With such exceptions, we must obey the powers under which we are constituted, because they derive their authority from God, even though they exercise it improperly. Christian obedience is moreover an infused moral virtue ; it is incomprehensible if it be not related to absolutely supernatural motives. Through the whole range of created hierarchies its obedience is rendered to God, it understands that the order and counsel received depend from that obscure government of Providence which makes use of human infirmities to serve some greater good.

In the case of a direction or a *counsel* as in the case of an *express order*—given by a lawful superior acting within the scope of his lawful authority—the virtue of obedience should come into play : but in different ways, broadly in the former, narrowly in the latter case. As there is, in fact, a correspondence between agent and patient, so there ought to be a correspondence between the manner in which the superior gradates the exercise of his authority and the manner in which the inferior gradates his docility.

11. If it is of the essence of a counsel not to require strict obedience and if, therefore, the inferior may have valid reasons for not executing materially whatever the superior more or less instantly suggests to or requires from him, there is, nevertheless, even so, a providential direction in the action of the superior which an intelligent obedience can distinguish and retain. This is a particularly complex and shifting domain, as always when prudence has to submit human contingencies to its regulations, which vary in every case. The essential then is the practical firmness of the filial dispositions of the will. There are filial acts of initiative and opposition which, so far from offending obedience, rather on the contrary presuppose it and are possible only through it, for they imply the profound docility of a mind rightly convinced that it is not disobedient and genuinely disposed to compliance if the authority (assuming always a lawful authority keeping within the bounds of its jurisdiction) transformed the counsel into a formal order. As a certain chill and excessively cautious fear, such as the fear with which Bossuet taxed Descartes in regard to the

Church, in reality borders close on disobedience, being a lifeless obedience, so liberty of feelings and confidence betoken a living, filial obedience.

Invited to take proceedings with his regal authority against people whose quarrels with their bishops involved questions of merely temporal interest, St. Louis, in refusing such requests, had no idea of setting up as a principle a superiority of his jurisdiction over that of the episcopate ; he merely wanted to be certain, for the tranquillity of his conscience, that his coercive measures would be just and in the first instance laughingly to evade " in his common sense," as Joinville says, claims he had some reason for thinking ill-founded. It is true that with regard to the Pope, the highest superior of all and judge without appeal, greater docility is required : for a number of prelates do not constitute the Church and do not bind the Church, as the judges of Rouen have clearly proved ; whereas the Pope is the authentic voice of the Church. Nevertheless, even as regards the Pope, intervening with a request or a counsel, St. Louis could display, without offence to the virtue of obedience, the liberty of a son [56]. If he refused the request of Gregory IX and Innocent IV to make war on Frederick II, first excommunicated and then deposed, his understanding with the Pope was in no way impaired ; he protected him at the Council of Lyons, placed himself at the Pope's disposal in an endeavour to effect a reconciliation between him and the Emperor and in the end violently threatened the latter that he would take the field against him [57]. It must however be observed that once the Pope expressly alleges as a reason for his intervention dangers which with our connivance might imperil the good of souls, the integrity of Catholic doctrine or devotion, the case would then assume a special gravity and require from us particularly effective and particularly prompt evidence of obedience.

It is for the Christian intelligence, the spirit of faith, the gift of counsel, to distinguish the providential directions referred to and to appreciate in every case the extent, importance and urgency of the docility required.

The absence of a filial impulse towards the Vicar of Christ, the fact of whittling away the counsel received to the utmost possible (there have been many cases of the sort in the last fifty years) will indicate precisely the absence or diminution of the spirit of faith. I have already recalled elsewhere the teaching on this point of Père Clérissac. " He declared that it was always possible, even when no express command intervened, to distinguish the pure spiritual line according to which the direction imposed from above became incumbent upon the virtue of obedience. He added that such exceeding deference for authority required also the nicest discernment, according to the degrees and kinds of subordination and mandate, for it related to a living and free docility of the practical judgement, not to a servile and mechanical performance. In spite of his attachment to his monarchical convictions, he deeply regretted that French Catholics should have been so disobedient, as he said, to Pope Leo XIII, and he blamed indifferently one party for not having shown sufficient obedience and the other for having gone beyond what an intelligent and filial obedience required. How many more examples might he not have adduced of such failures to obey *in spirit and truth* the will of the Pope " [58].

12. If, such being the case, the Church gives not merely a counsel or direction, but a categorical order, then it is clear that we owe her obedience, not only in the spirit but also in the letter of the order received ; it is a *fault* not to obey strictly.

What sort of fault ? As far as the direct power of the Church over spiritual things is concerned, we commit a fault against faith [1] in not conforming our judgement to an *infallible doctrinal decision*, whether it proceed from a definition or solemn condemnation *ex cathedra* or the ordinary and universal magistracy of the Church [59] ; we commit a sin of doctrinal temerity, a fault against the obedience due to the Church so far as interior assent itself is concerned, in refusing either a *doctrinal* instruction imparted by the Pope with the general assistance of the Holy Ghost, but not involving any infallible decision, or a non-infallible *doctrinal* decision determining the better opinion in any particular matter connected with the Faith [60] ; we also commit a fault against obedience in resisting an order given by the Church in virtue of its direct power in the sphere of *spiritual government* and *discipline* [61]. Lastly, we commit a fault against obedience, a fault against the justice and the filial piety which bind us to the Church in resisting an order given by the Church in virtue of her *indirect power over the temporal* [62]. The mystic Body of Christ forms a

---

[1] A truth (in doctrine or of fact) may be *infallibly* proposed either as *of revelation* or merely as *connected with* revealed dogma. The obstinate refusal to give one's adhesion is a fault against faith which the Church in the former case describes as *heresy*.

perfect society, that is to say an absolutely self-sufficient community lacking none of the elements which together constitute social life ; a perfect society presupposes an authority to which obedience is due in conscience, even where that authority is fallible.

The Pope can, no doubt, change his mind when the subject matter is fallible and contingent. One Pope can undo the work of a predecessor. So that a filial obedience is bound to submit, under pain of fault, to the command once given and under pain of imperfect conformity to the spiritual line which the Christian intelligence can discern in the command or the mere counsel—but it is nevertheless legitimate, if one has good reasons therefor, to try to induce the Pope to change his decision, as a son may in the case of his father, the father in this case being the supreme authority on earth.

Once the order is issued, however, there is no option but to obey.

We should always remember that there is normally a presumption of right in favour of the superior and that nothing is so unreasonable, in the event of being oneself called upon to obey, as to go and ransack history for a collection of precedents of mistakes made by authority. That kind of zeal does not argue enlightenment. Nevertheless a precise theory of obedience ought to define the obligations below which, in default of a more generous virtue, it is strictly speaking impossible to go. Although as a general rule it is rash to express even an interior speculative judgement *contrary* to the judgement of the supreme superior, who is more enlightened than any one else and has the general interests of the Church in mind, nevertheless conformity of the speculative judgement is not required, even with respect to an order from the Pope, at all events so long as the Pope is not speaking *ex cathedra* or does not have recourse to measures such as encyclicals, for example, or the doctrinal decrees of the Holy Office which oblige our interior assent [63]. But even when it is possible for the speculative judgement to remain in suspense the practical judgement and the will ought to conform to the order given. " Even unjust censures are to be received with respect," said Gregory the Great, " for in resisting them, we run the risk, by our very pride of disobedience, of giving rise to the fault which until then was non-existent " [64].

It is of the highest importance in this connection to understand the peculiar character of the obedience due to a reality which, like the Church of Christ, itself constitutes a supernatural mystery ; the Church is not only a visible and apparent reality but also an object of faith, not a system of administrative cog-wheels but the Body of Christ whose living unity, incomparably more elevated and stronger than anything in this world we describe as moral personality, is guaranteed by the action of the Holy Ghost. If the men who visibly exercise authority therein act as responsible agents,[1] liable as such to human error (except in cases involving infallibility), they nevertheless act as agents subordinate to the government of Jesus Christ, the invisible Head of the whole body. Not only do the practical errors of judgement and any other mistakes they may make become incorporated, as foreseen and permitted, in that divine government of the Church,

[1] Cf. pp. 7-8.

but also, even so, at any rate where the decisions of the supreme visible chief are concerned, the wisdom of the Spirit of Christ makes the universal Church tend positively, through all the hesitations and infirmities of her humanity, to ends which are always just and good. The faithful heart is well aware that, in the mystic Body of Christ, the shortcomings of human nature still serve the most holy action of God, which never fails to attain its goal.

I do not hereby intend to palliate such weaknesses or abuses as have occurred in the course of time. I would, on the contrary, rather emphasise them, but whatever displeasure they may have given God, whatever providential sanctions they may have earned, they have never diverted the Church from her end. The assistance of the Holy Ghost guarantees her not only a simple and as it were negative privilege of inerrancy in matters of faith (a privilege which ought to be regarded on the contrary as the consequence of the most active and elevated intellectual gift) [65], but also a positive direction, an irresistible progressive movement which derives profit from everything, shortcomings and errors no less than feats of strength and virtues, and which, even when the subject matter is fallible, subordinates every decision of the supreme authority to a divinely just and true intention [66]. Our speculative judgement can and ought always to adhere in faith to that intention of the Holy Ghost, even though it be imperceptible to our eyes of flesh. And this very fact makes the conformity of the practical judgement and the will incomparably easier in regard to the Church and the Pope than in regard to any other authority [67].

13. Leaving merely theoretical considerations for the contemplation of facts, such conformity of the practical judgement is all the easier because, in reality, as a general rule, an impartial examination of the particular circumstances compels the admission that the decisions of the pontifical government appear in the majority of cases on the whole more just and far better founded than that of any other. As regards the censures—even the non-infallible censures—with which the Popes, for the defence of Catholic doctrine or spirit, have visited certain great currents of thought, they have always condemned evils which were only too real. Nevertheless, with the exception of cases of infallible definition, where the prudential contingencies of practical opportunities were concerned, errors and deficiencies inseparable from human government have not always been avoided. " The power which has never abused its strength does not exist," wrote Joseph de Maistre, observing, also, that in fact the history of the Papacy, considered as a whole, has an incomparably better record than any other human principality and gives " the mind of every intelligent observer the impression of a power palpably receiving assistance." " It is not a question of whether the Popes were men or if they never made mistakes " [68], either spontaneously or because they were badly or insufficiently informed. Any historian can pass any judgement he likes on any of their acts, his judgement lacks authority and is invalid. Once they gave orders, they had to be obeyed. Saints such as St. Irenaeus and St. Catharine of Siena might address violent remonstrances to them. They none the less obeyed [69]. Placed on the pinnacle of spiritual sovereignty,

they depend on no created authority. For the good or evil use they make of their power, they are responsible to God alone : to Him alone they are accountable for whatever practical errors or abuses they may commit ; according to the magnificent analogy drawn by the old theologians, " the spiritual man judgeth all things : and he himself is judged of no man." [1] " Therefore, if terrestrial authority goes astray, it will be judged by the spiritual authority. If the lower spiritual authority goes astray, it will be judged by the higher spiritual authority, and if the supreme spiritual authority goes astray, it can be judged by God alone and not by man " [70]. He who, as regards the State, stands on the summit of spirituality, is not amenable to the judgement of any man. "Take care," said St. Catharine of Siena to Gregory XI, " that I do not have to complain about you to Jesus crucified. There is no one else I can complain to, for you have no superior on earth."

To allege on any particular occasion when the Pope exercises his indirect power that he is transgressing the limits of his lawful authority and then to pretend, as an excuse for non-obedience, an abuse of authority in the juridical sense of the term is an absurdity, for the reason that a power is concerned whose sphere of activity does not admit of any predetermined limits and the extent of the application of which it is for the Pope alone to determine in any particular case. It is sufficient that the Pope should consider that a sufficiently serious spiritual interest is involved in any temporal arrangement for an intervention by him in

[1] St. Paul, 1 Corinthians ii. 15. This text is quoted by Boniface VIII in the Bull *Unam sanctam*.

regard thereto to be legitimate. The same rule clearly applies, and *a fortiori*, to reactions on the temporal of a measure itself falling within the province of the direct power (doctrinal and disciplinary) over the spiritual.

To apply the teaching of St. Thomas with regard to obedience to human laws [71], resistance would appear to be permissible in two cases only : (*a*) in the event of a Pope taking steps plainly subversive of the common good of the Church and (*b*) in the event of his ordering the commission of a sin, the performance of an intrinsically evil act, in which case disobedience would not merely be permissible but even necessary. Such cases, however, have never occurred in the government of the Church by its visible Head acting as such. If among many good and saintly Popes there have been some few bad, they have never set up their own faults as laws of the Church or perverted those laws to their own advantage. Never, in addressing the Church with the express intention of binding the faithful, have they ordered evil to be done. If a Pope, acting as a private person or issuing an order to some individual, may occasionally place a soul in a situation to commit sin, the Vicar of Christ, acting as Head of the Church, is nevertheless by divine right *the certain guide of human life* [72] ; it is impossible—for the gates of Hell would then prevail—for any of his universal disciplinary decrees [73] ever to enjoin anything contrary to what is morally good [74] ; theologians, no doubt, do not admit the same impossibility in the case of decisions lacking the validity of universal law ; to have the right, however, not to obey one of them, it must appear immediately, self-evidently and incontestably opposed to the law of God,[1] and the instances they adduce are all entirely theoretical acts of monstrous wickedness : of a Pope refusing to grant an ecclesiastical benefice except against payment in gold, transforming St. Peter's in Rome into a palace for his relations, ordering the treasure of the Church to be distributed among them and so forth. . . . In fact, God has never permitted the conscience of the Faithful to be divided between a commandment of His and a formal obligation imposed by the Pope in virtue of his apostolic authority ; even when practical errors, ill considered or inopportune actions may creep in, the Church is still protected against everything which would be radically contrary to her mission.

One would therefore be running grave risk of condemning oneself, by showing that one entertained very hazardous opinions concerning the Church and

[1] Cf. in this connection the answers given by Bellarmine to the "seven madmen of Venice," as he described the seven theologians who claimed to justify the resistance of the Senate of Venice to a brief of Paul V. On the 17th April, 1606, Paul V—for legitimate reasons— had laid Venice under an interdict. "The Senate of Venice refused to admit the Pope's brief and had a public protest billed against what it had the temerity to call a void and null document ; then, in order to allay the agitation of minds, it appointed a committee of theologians with instructions to prove the justice of these steps and the illegality of the interdict " (Couderc, *le Vénérable Cardinal Bellarmin*, 1893, vol. i, p. 110). Bellarmine replied to the memorial of these theologians in two *Riposte* in which he gives a practical commentary of his *De Summo Pontifice* (Fèvre, vol. viii). " If the sin is evident," he wrote, " there is no duty to obey and it is idle to examine things which are self-evident : if the sin is doubtful, obedience is a duty and one can refer to the judgement of a superior ; a subject is not thereby exposed to the risk of sin : because God commands him to obey his superior, so that, if there be any sin in such obedience, the superior will bear the blame and the subject take the merit." Fra Paolo Sarpi, who was chiefly responsible for the memorial, had written that, before obeying any order received even from the Supreme Pontiff, Christians ought first to consider whether the order was proper, lawful and binding. Bellarmine replied that that was a heretical opinion, because it condemned and declared

the Pope, if one were to allege such pretexts as a reason for disobeying a categorical order of the Church or the Pope. If the Pope, for the defence of Catholic doctrine or the integrity of the Christian spirit, issued a decree calling upon some school of thought or political party to reform itself—to allege that he is ordering the commission of a sin, because such a party cannot reform itself without ceasing to exist and the country will be " assassinated " if it ceases to exist, would not only be proceeding to an unheard of reversal of values, by making the *status quo* of a party in practice a good superior to the good of souls and the Church ; it would also involve making the most serious decision possible depend upon a non-existent principle and having recourse to the right of resistance in the very case in which such a right did not come

blameworthy the simple unquestioning obedience commended by all the Fathers and the Holy Ghost Himself. To question a command not clearly involving a sin is reprehended by the Fathers, because anyone who submits the command to his own scrutiny thereby appoints himself the judge of his superior and St. James says : " *if thou judge the law, thou art not a doer of the law but a judge.*" " This is the twelfth proposition in the tract of the seven theologians and it is heretical. . . . For simple unquestioning obedience of the order is commended by all the holy Fathers and by the Holy Spirit Himself, Ps. xvii " . . . " *at the hearing of the ear, they have obeyed me,*" i.e. as soon as they heard, they obeyed at once without further question. But Fr. Paul's proposition . . . condemns the same obedience as evil and makes the obedient guilty of sin. But the questioning of a command which does not clearly involve a sin is reprehended by the Fathers, because anyone questioning the precept appoints himself judge of his superior " and Bellarmine then quotes St. James (cf. *Auctarium Bellarminum*, ed. Le Bachelet, No. 87, § 2, p. 588).

Bellarmine, in his second answer, repeats that a mere probability is not enough to warrant disobedience and recalls the general rule laid down by St. Augustine that the subject is bound to obey not only when he is sure that the superior is ordering him nothing against God, but also when he is not certain if he is ordering him something against God, because in case of doubt it is his duty to follow the judgement of the superior and not his own (*Riposta ad un libretto*, etc. Fèvre, vol. viii, p. 64).

into play : for would anyone dare to suggest that such a series of equations is immediately evident and undeniably possible ? Even to such as do not perceive its indubitable falsity, it cannot but appear as eminently debatable. Now as Bellarmine, recalling St. Augustine, reminds us, to question an order received which does not *clearly* involve a sin is to constitute the subject judge of the superior ; one would be entitled to refuse obedience to the Pope only if his command appeared clearly and beyond all shadow of doubt contrary to the law of God. " A mere probability is not enough. The subject is bound to obey, not only when he is sure that the superior is not ordering him something contrary to God, but also when he is not certain that he is ordering him something contrary to God, because in case of doubt he must follow the judgement of the superior and not his own judgement. . . . He does not then run the risk of committing sin, because God has ordered him to obey his superior, so that if there be anything wrong in such obedience, the fault is the fault of the superior and the merit the merit of the subject." [1]

14. Obedience always does harm to something ; it is a sacrifice. Instead of going to fetch Placid and walking on the waters, Maurus might have retorted to St. Benedict that to throw oneself into the water without being able to swim was to sin against the duty of self-preservation, which is a natural right. There would always be good reasons for disobedience on that score and every sacrifice would appear as a sin. In reality to suffer some detriment to oneself or to what one

[1] Cf. the preceding note.

loves for a superior good is not sinful, but meritorious. If the superior commands an act forbidden by God, obedience in that case would be a sin. But it is not a sin against the duties which we owe ourselves to obey our country when it asks us to risk our life for it. Similarly it is no sin to risk any terrestrial good whatever, however eminent, to obey the Church. For the good to which the Church is ordered and in virtue of which the Pope commands is eternal life. There is no greater good. Duty to the State or their country has as a rule been alleged by nations and kings as a pretext for rebellion against the power of the Church. But one's country is not above God, the good of the human State is not above the good of the divine State. The Church, that is to say Christ, takes precedence of our country in the hierarchy of our love [75]. Besides, as a matter of fact, if we love one above the other, we need have no fear that God will ask us to choose between them. Such a sacrifice has never been required except and through its own fault from the Jewish people, which unconsciously achieved it and so doing ruined itself for the redemption of the world.

May it not sometimes happen, however, that in giving an order for the protection of the spiritual, the Pope may, in certain cases, gravely compromise temporal interests which ought to be dear to us? To proceed at once to the extreme, let us suppose such a case. Well then, if we think so, we can make representations to the Pope exposing the gravity of the circumstances and try to induce him to change his decision. But we must obey.

No private person, no temporal authority, prince

or emperor, is appointed judge of the universal good, is entitled to have his private judgement prevail in the government of things over the order issued by the Head of the Church on account of spiritual interests. And if the Pope does not change his mind, if grave temporal interests are really thereby endangered, we must still obey, although we may contrive, by every honourable means compatible with obedience, to protect such interests. And have recourse to God. It is the only recourse then possible.

In fact, I hasten to add, things will never reach such an extremity. Why? Because in obeying a superior in the exercise of his lawful authority—even *supposing* that the act ordered, without being itself bad, runs the risk of injuring by its consequences very sacred interests—we are obeying God. God permits it for the superior ends of His special providence which is in the highest degree universal. The palpable and immediate inconveniences then resulting from obedience are the condition of some future good, assuring in their most real significance, by some unpredictable reversal, the grave interests in question ; for the Providence of man can and ought only to judge according to such knowledge as it can possess, whereas the Providence of God judges according to the secrets concealed within it, according to the real state, imperceptible to our eyes, of human forces and minds, lastly but not least, by taking account of the *fortuitous* which depends on that Providence alone. If the interests in question are as just and sacred as they are thought to be, it will surely take care of them. This doctrine may seem harsh, because it puts the invisible before the visible. For anyone who believes in God and the supernatural order, it is more certain than a mathematical demonstration.

It is not based upon the general justice of Providence only, but also, as far as one's country in particular is concerned, on the very nature of the political community and its good. For all things in the universe are ordered. And the terrestrial State being ordered by nature, as we have seen, to the moral good of the human being, and therefore necessarily ordered in fact to eternal life as to its last end and to the good of the divine State, it is a metaphysical impossibility for the terrestrial State to attain its peculiar end and true prosperity in opposition to the good of the Church. Yet it believed that it could. The history of the modern world is the history of that illusion. The results are before our eyes.

The preceding hypothesis was therefore illegitimate. In fact, obedience to the orders of the Church can never compromise to any permanent and profound extent temporal interests which ought to be dear to us, more particularly the interests of the State. It can injure only certain momentary aspects and above all *our conception* of those interests. For we constantly tend to confuse the public good with the way in which we want to ensure it. But nobody has the right to identify his private cause with the cause and common good of the country.

V. THE TEMPORAL SOVEREIGNTY OF THE POPE

15. The temporal sovereignty of the Pope is a different thing from his indirect power over the tem-

poral, but it follows from the same principles, that is to say from the primacy of the spiritual over the temporal and the connection between the two.

It is absolutely necessary that the spiritual sovereignty, that is to say the supreme sovereignty, shall be perfectly free and independent : that the person invested with it therefore be *subject* to no temporal power or any State. But no other means has yet been or ever will be devised of not being subject unless to be *sovereign*. The Pope, therefore, must absolutely be a temporal sovereign [76], because of his spiritual sovereignty. This temporal sovereignty is attached to his person : he is a royal person, the most eminent of all. The Papal States and the kingship he formerly wielded over them were at once the symbol and the guarantee of that sovereignty : the Vatican City is so now.

The Pope, as a temporal sovereign, has a diplomatic service as formerly he had an army. He has a temporal policy which is directed, no doubt, in the character he impresses upon it, to the preservation of spiritual interests, but which, of itself, remains distinct from his indirect power, his right to intervene at any point in the temporal sphere by a counsel or a command because of those same interests. And as his army once conformed to military custom and sometimes even waged war, so his diplomatic service conforms to the customs and methods of the chancellories, without thereby requiring—although the most respectful deference is naturally due to it—the obedience of the nations.

So at the same time as in the plenitude of his universal spiritual sovereignty, which makes him everywhere at home, he acts as supreme judge directly over the spiritual and indirectly over the temporal because of spiritual interests, the Pope exercises in the world, in virtue of his temporal sovereignty, a purely political activity ordered to the spiritual good of Christendom but of a merely diplomatic kind.

It is important to distinguish between this merely political action, which leaves us free agents, and orders issued in virtue of the direct or indirect power, which would have us obedient.

II

A CRISIS OF THE CATHOLIC SPIRIT

I. THE CONDEMNATION OF THE ACTION FRANCAISE

16. A GRAVE crisis involving some of the essential principles of religion and the most pressing problems of the day occurred a few years ago among the Catholics of France with reference to the Action Française and the warnings issued in regard to it by the Holy See. The movement was subsequently condemned. In a pamphlet published at the beginning of the crisis, I proposed to examine the political thought of Maurras, indicating both the partial truths implicit in it and the dangers it involved. The pamphlet concluded with an appeal to filial obedience which alone in a crisis, the gravity of which was everywhere realised, could prevent more stringent sanctions [77].

Subsequent events have greatly modified and enlarged the significance of the crisis in quite a different sense from what might have been desired ; the conclusions imposed on the debate by the course of events now need to be recorded. It is the business of ecclesiastical authority to explain the motives and the grounds of the condemnations it decrees and I do not propose to trespass upon its domain. In reverting to a painful incident, my intention is merely to discern its meaning and moral and above all to anticipate some of the conditions of the positive work which remains to be done.

I repeat here what I said in the pamphlet above mentioned ; urged by overwhelming moral evidence, I intervene simply in order to testify to the truth, by setting forth the considered opinion of an impartial onlooker ; I speak only for myself. I may be permitted to express the hope that the reader will consent to forget for a moment the bitterness engendered by a recent past and all controversy on matters of detail so that the question may be considered in a universal aspect. If I could obtain from some that " silence in Heaven about the space of half an hour " mentioned in the Apocalypse, I should consider myself fortunate. I am well aware that neither the violence of passionate discussions nor the apathy which allows wounds to go septic of themselves is capable of providing any remedy for evils latent in the conflict and constituting a danger to the souls of individuals and the welfare of my country and that they are only to be cured by light ; I would collaborate above all to the best of my poor ability with the interior work of such as are resolved to raise themselves by an effort of the mind above time.

I can only think of Charles Maurras with sorrow. Devoured with a passion for order and the supreme laws of authority, he was then to be seen at the head of Catholics, who defied the orders of their spiritual Chief and lay under the ban of the supreme authority which in his heart he never ceased to revere, although the secret of its essential nature and its inspiration escape him. The affection I bear that indomitable soul makes me realise the full tragedy of his destiny.

But the love I bear the Vicar of the crucified God

45

makes me also realise the depth of his personal, his paternal suffering. He has charge of the whole world. If he strikes, it is for the good of souls, to heal the wounds of Christ's flock. In the awful solitude which raises him above all men, all the sorrows of Christendom are echoed in him ; he acts as the faithful shepherd, he risks himself for love of us, goaded by the consciousness of his responsibilities. Of the multitude of Christians moved by every kind of human sentiment, how many give a thought to the sorrows of the Pope, to the great anguish ever vigilant on the top of the towers of the Church ?

17. The Church, no doubt, intended to intervene in the present quarrel in virtue simply of her doctrinal magistracy and to censure authoritatively certain errors, a system of ideas described by the Pope as " political, doctrinal and practical modernism " [1] ; such intervention was within the province of her direct power over the spiritual and the protection of the spiritual was the determining factor in the disciplinary measures so taken. At the same time, however—and precisely because the party thereby affected devoted itself mainly to political activity and played an important part in the political life of its country—the connection between the spiritual and the temporal became involved. This caused many people great distress. The object of this book is not to examine the doctrines of the Action Française, but to recall with reference to recent events the laws governing the

[1] Cf. the Letter of Pope Pius XI to Cardinal Andrieu of the 5th January, 1927. The condemnation of a certain number of works by Charles Maurras also falls within the jurisdiction of the direct (doctrinal and disciplinary) power.

primacy of the spiritual, and it will therefore be confined to that aspect of the problem. Considered from that point of view, what was the problem raised by, the core of the difficulty in, the condemnation of the Action Française ?

The condemnation of the Action Française, a political, not a religious party, was in fact a blow struck at the temporal order ; but its motive and formal object were to ward off dangers of a spiritual order [1] which the Church, by the voice of the Pope, declared to be latent in that group. There was a repercussion of doctrinal and disciplinary measures on the temporal domain, less directly affected and certainly less seriously than when the Pope deposed an emperor or a king. The condemnation was decreed on account of spiritual interests of which the Pope is the sole supreme judge. It is clear that the only possible attitude for the Catholic conscience to adopt was obedience at the cost of whatever sacrifices.

I do not say that such obedience was easy for many of those who belonged to the Action Française. To deny or belittle the amount of suffering or the severity of the ordeal thereby imposed upon them would be most unjust. Its supporters had given their adhesion to that political school for reasonable and disinterested motives, the defence of their country against a corrosive anarchy begotten of the party system and the restoration of a political and national order which seemed to involve even the good of souls. Some had even done so with the sole object of serving the Church

---

[1] " A danger both to the integrity of faith and morals and to the Catholic education of youth." Pope Pius XI, Consistorial address of the 20th December. 1926.

in what they considered the most effective way and they had offered the leaders of the Action Française an ardent devotion and on occasion an admirable spirit of self-sacrifice. In difficult circumstances they had loyally and effectively served the cause of religion. They were frequently told that they were, and they sometimes described themselves as, the best Catholics in France. In a few months they saw themselves surrounded with suspicion. Not only were there charitable souls then found, as there always are in such cases, to pour vinegar into their wounds in all disinterestedness, but they hardly understood the motives behind the suspicion surrounding them. The terms of certain accusations, at all events in the beginning of the affair, seemed to accuse them of crimes of which they felt innocent.

What is important in an ordeal is the manner in which it is borne. A trial—by definition—is sent to test the characters of men.

God, Who tempts nobody beyond his strength, may suddenly call upon any Christian to act like a hero. He then grants proportionate graces. Hundreds and hundreds of poor Chinese peasants at the time of the Boxer persecutions were suddenly faced with the choice between martyrdom and apostasy ; they chose martyrdom. There was no question of martyrdom in the present case : merely a sacrifice and an act of humility. Obedience might have been tinged with heroism in the case of such as were ignorant of the reasons determining the pontifical intervention, but the opportunity of proving one's love does not occur every day. It must also be observed that the action taken by the Church was in this case less severe in the beginning than in others ; the Church proceeded by successive steps with intervals of delay which the spirit of obedience could have turned to account.

" It has been said," wrote Père Clérissac [78], " that we must be able to suffer not only on behalf of the Church, but also at the hands of the Church. If there be any truth in the observation, it is that we sometimes need to be hardly dealt with, to be kept in the shade, in silence, with every appearance of disgrace, because we have not perhaps derived sufficient holy profit from the favours and advances of the Church at other times." He added that it must " never be admitted that we can possibly suffer at the hands of the Church otherwise than at the hands of God."

The question then arises : Was it a *servile* and *passive* obedience which was required in the case under consideration ? Not in the least ; but a supernatural obedience, that is to say a *filial* obedience to the visible Head of the Body of Christ, and an *intelligent* obedience with the intelligence which derives from the spirit of faith [79]. The rules, gradations and obligations of such obedience have been recalled in the *exposé* of doctrine contained in the first chapter of this book.

Obedience did not imply that to give the Pope every guarantee he might require for the preservation of Catholic doctrine and the Catholic spirit (he being the sole judge of the extent of such guarantee) was thereby to abdicate legitimate freedom in the remaining purely political sphere and to be obliged in conscience to conform to every temporal direction of pontifical diplomacy, whose suggestions it is always as absurd to despise as it is shameful to calumniate its objects, motives being naturally subject to the ordinary contingencies of the play of political forces.

Obedience did not oblige, as has been alleged, " to call white what was seen to be black " ; did not oblige to subscribe, as to formulae binding the mind of every single person, to every proposition contained in Cardinal Andrieu's two letters. What it essentially required was conformity of the practical judgement and conduct to the orders received from the Sovereign Pontiff. And it also presupposed—and this is the specific characteristic of supernatural obedience to the Church—the conviction that, *even in fallible things*, and whatever the human element may be in the exterior presentation of things, a pure ray of the spirit which is all justice and all truth is transmitted in every act of the Pope when he issues a command as Head of the Church, in other words in every act of the Universal Church, even though at the first glance we are unable to perceive so much as a gleam. Humility then quickly discovers in the interior light of God the recondite reasons for what at first, in the exterior light of human events, may have been felt to be insufficiently founded.

Obedience was not a surrender to the designs of any particular opponent without authority, but simply to the will of the Pope acting in the plenitude of his powers. There always have been and there ever will be human rivalries whose importance as regards the divine elements prevailing in the conduct of the Church will always be exaggerated. Loyal hearts were distressed because they confused the order of the Church and the Pope with the hopes of certain political enemies eager to exploit the situation. Such distress betokened great short-sightedness.

Because the truth of the practical judgement must be considered in relation to the integrity of the will or love, an impulse of the heart often simplifies the most complicated human problems. If you love the Church, you love the Pope, not in an abstract, ineffective way, but practically, as the living image of Christ in our midst. If you love the Pope, you are under no temptation to misprize him, you trust him, you traverse in a step all human intermediaries to make yourself one with the apostolic intentions; " If you love the Pope," said Pius X, " you do not stop to debate what he counsels or requires, to discover the extent of the strict duty of obedience and determine the limits of its obligation. If you love the Pope, you do not object that he has not spoken sufficiently clearly, as though he were obliged to repeat directly into the ear of everyone the desire he has so often clearly expressed, not only in speech but also in letters and other public documents ; you do not cast doubt upon his orders on the facile pretext of the wilfully disobedient that they do not proceed directly from him, but from his entourage ; you do not try to circumscribe the area in which he may and ought to exercise his authority, you do not oppose the authority of other persons, however learned, whose opinion differs from the Pope's against the authority of the Pope . . ." [80]. Pius XI prays for France daily and offers his Masses for France. He intervened with regard to the Action Française only after convincing himself, by a personal examination, that the care of many souls made it his strict duty. His conscience as chief pastor is at stake in the quarrel.

If we bear all this in mind, there is less chance of our practical judgement going astray.

There are times when all the voices of our neighbours lie, noisily telling us *non ea quae Dei sunt, sed ea quae hominum.* The soul is then alone and Christ instructs it from within, repelling such voices as emanating from the devil, even though they proceed from the lips of ecclesiastical teachers and theologians. "You are suffering injustice," the voices cried. All the more reason for obedience, obedience being precisely the way in which to have the justice of God on your side. "They want to kill you," the voices cried. All the more reason for obedience ; obedience disarms wrath and the common Father of all does not kill children who throw themselves into his arms. The Pope, in fact, had not condemned the Action Française movement because it was monarchist or national ; he had, on the contrary, made an express reservation of freedom for Catholics to choose any particular form of government they liked and try to establish it by every honourable means [81]. In this, as in every similar case, the Church intervened merely in order to preserve the spiritual good and was fully determined to maintain, if the required guarantees were forthcoming, the legitimate political independence of the faithful which is not merely theoretical or platonic, because it is defined and may one day find itself subject to restrictions of varying gravity, but remains practical and effective. It was not the duty of the Church to indicate to the Action Française Catholics how they should continue to exercise such political freedom, while accommodating themselves to the guarantees required of them, nor was it the duty of the Pope to discover a means of preserving whatever good there was in the movement. It is hardly conceivable that a party which aspired to the direction of French politics should not have had sufficient elasticity and ingenuity to devise solutions capable of according its own political activity with all that obedience required. Besides, it is common knowledge that whoever fights the Church ends by being defeated. Such an encounter should have been avoided at all costs by anyone desirous of preserving the work which had been undertaken. Obedience might perhaps have secured a mitigation of sentence. Disobedience made the aggravation of it inevitable. In any event, from the supernatural point of view of the spirit of faith as from the simple point of view of political prudence, it seemed that only a great impulse of confident and generous obedience (not excluding the filial exposition of what was considered proper and desirable, but requiring a heart submitting unreservedly and hoping against hope) could restore the situation in such a crisis. It is a great theme for meditation in thinking of the prestige the Action Française had the opportunity of acquiring, if it had realised such things, to reflect that God permitted that it should not realise them.

In fact, after the protestation of faith by its directors and Catholic student members, the Action Française assumed a correct and silent attitude—savouring rather of immobility under the blow than alacrity to examine itself ; then a violent campaign of controversy began in the press, and qualified proposals were made as between equal powers (it had already presented a justification couched in the most exalted terms in the letter addressed by Charles Maurras to the Sovereign

Pontiff,[1] but with nothing which recalled the *Domine, quid me vis facere* of St. Paul to Christ) ; when the condemnation finally arrived,[2] it resolved on open opposition to the authority of the Church,[3] and polemical methods which speedily involved its being placed on the Index.[4]

18. The Action Française had so encountered on its path the stone which saves or causes stumbling ; it was faced with a choice in which the supernatural spirit ought clearly to have been predominant. The choice made was erroneous. It is the less surprising, if we bear in mind the principle that a community, as such, can never do more than its leader. In the present case the leader, being himself an infidel, felt bound in conscience to refuse. At the gravest moment of its destiny, the political community of the Action Française so found itself deprived of those supreme decisions which the leader alone can take in his solitude before God. It was left to itself and, however deeply religious the feelings of many of its members considered as individuals may have been, *as a community* it had no more exalted spring of action than the spirit it derived from its leader.

We are here in the core of the drama. We see why the Church has always regarded it as a very fearful

[1] Letter dated the 12th October, 1926, first published on the 20th February, 1927.

[2] Official note of the *Osservatore Romano*, 15th December, 1926 ; Consistorial address *Misericordia Domini*, 20th December, 1926.

[3] *Non possumus*, Action Française of the 24th December, 1926.

[4] Decree of the Holy Office condemning certain works of Charles Maurras and the newspaper *L'Action Française* dated the 29th January, 1914, and the 29th December, 1926. The personal intervention of the Supreme Pontiff gives this decree a special gravity. (Cf. Lucien Choupin, *Valeur des décisions doctrinales et disciplinaires du Saint-Siège*, 3rd ed., Paris, 1928.)

danger that a Christian nation should be governed by an infidel king. The Church has been violently and bitterly required to give the reasons for her severity towards the Action Française. One was enough and in my opinion remains the most profound ; the Action Française was a party which associated many Catholics, more particularly a considerable number of young men, in a political community (political I say, not religious or philosophical), placed as such under the absolute intellectual direction of an infidel leader. This was an entirely different thing from a mere collaboration with non-Catholics. It raised the question of the head. However scrupulously careful Charles Maurras may have been not to communicate his own philosophical and religious ideas to his friends and disciples—it is important to bear him this testimony and indeed their faithful devotion or return to the practice of their religion was a special source of joy and pride to him—a more subtle danger remained. Not only was there a risk of the error becoming widespread in spite of everything, through imponderable influences, in that secluded sphere of philosophical or religious conceptions ; but also and above all, in the very sphere of the science and practice of the good government of the State—if it be true that a proper and complete idea of the State and civil authority necessarily acknowledges as their first principle the law of God as the Author of the natural order and the rights of the Redeemer [1] ; if it be consequently true that a complete political science is not only philosophical but also theological and that the only good system of politics is purely and simply a Christian system [2]—

[1] Cf. Leo XIII's Encyclical, *Immortale Dei*.   [2] Cf. Appendix II.

it was to be feared that in a political community under the guidance of an infidel head, the defects of the latter might contaminate the body of the community in such a way as to distort the Christian sense and a non-Catholic or semi-Catholic way of estimating the things of the State be insensibly and unconsciously developed in that political body. Something much more subtle than a mere doctrinal error is here involved—a state of mind. The Church, " which has in an eminent degree the grace which St. Paul describes as the discerning of spirits " [82], perceives in such a case, as though by some maternal instinct, the presence of a state of mind which is not that of her Master and then reacts against it with the sort of passionate anxiety which inspires mothers in fighting against an obscure, diffuse danger. Mothers then require their children the more imperiously to trust them, as they perceive them to be the less capable of themselves understanding, while they continue to be dominated by such a state of mind, the reasons provoking such anxiety.

It was not, however, difficult in itself to discern the dangers which the Church was anxious to oppose and which sprang from what may be called political naturalism [83] ; (for this reason anyone who had the will might have realised, after the first moments of surprise, the deep-seated reasons for the pontifical intervention). The appreciation of the gravity and imminence of such dangers might have excited discussion. It was for the Pope alone to form an authoritative judgement of the peril as of the sufficiency or insufficiency of the means proposed for warding it off.

What in fact was the degree of gravity? The judgement thereupon of the supreme head, the *provisor universalis*, was much more severe than that of many Catholics fighting in the plain and necessarily considering things from more personal points of view. Nothing was to manifest more clearly the state of affairs than events themselves ; they were destined, as Pius XI sadly said, " to reveal the thoughts of many minds." For my own part, I had considered that the risks of error to which attention was drawn could easily have been avoided. I was mistaken. Leaving out of the question many things which may be explained by reactions of pain or anger—such reactions are not permanent—there are features in the conduct adopted by the members of a political body as of a common personality, which indicate the dispositions engendered by the spirit animating the whole. In this particular it must be confessed the deception was great. We were offered the spectacle of many Catholics deliberately choosing open disobedience despite the obligations of justice and charity [1] which bind us to the Body of Christ and supreme unity, because they considered themselves unjustly condemned by the sovereign authority and believing every sort of invention concerning the intentions of the Sovereign Pontiff [84]. When the Pope declared in the most explicit personal terms [85] that his condemnation was for spiritual reasons, they had no hesitation in giving him the lie and declaring that he was in reality actuated by political considerations.

[1] Every division in the Church, St. Thomas teaches, is a sin against charity, because it is charity which constitutes unity. " And so the sin of schism is by itself a particular (special) sin, because its object is to make a separation from unity which is constituted by charity ; charity not only binds one person to another by a spiritual bond of love, but the whole Church also in the union of the spirit " (*Sum. Theol.*, ii–ii, 39, 1).

They were heard to protest in all sincerity that they were good Catholics, entirely subject to the Church in faith and morals, and yet they refused to submit to the Church when, speaking as the supreme judge of the interests of faith and morals, she indirectly condemned a political movement[1] ; they declared that the Pope, in intervening as head of the Church to forbid them to read a newspaper or be members of a political organisation, was ordering them to commit a sin against their country, " to murder their mother," without so much as noticing that it was a sin against their mother, the Church of Christ, to entertain such thoughts about her. To consider the question more deeply : would the scandal which many souls suffered when they believed, on seeing the Action Française condemned, that the cause of Catholicism itself and its spiritual values were compromised, have occurred, if a certain utterly rational conception of the Church, considered in the supererogatory benefits she confers upon us and as the custodian of social order and the Latin civilisation such as Maurras conceives them to be, had not in practice predominated in their minds over the supernatural adhesion by faith to what the Church essentially is : the mystic Body of Christ ? Would the drama of conscience which tortured them have been so cruel, if they had not judged the Church, by standards of utterly human prudence, as a power of this world whose supposed conflict with the mother country then became insoluble ?

Nor did they realise that it was entertaining a very

---

[1] A practical denial in the particular circumstances of the right of the spiritual power to intervene in the temporal in order to protect a spiritual good.

poor opinion of France, her natural resources and providential destiny, to think that any political party, however useful it might be deemed, was the country's *last chance of salvation*, or its *only means of salvation*, was, in a word, essential to its life as an indispensable means. I would add that if the way in which, for weeks on end, the Action Française represented its condemnation as dictated to the Church by a policy opposed to French interests, resulted in aggravating the burden on many consciences already in the circumstances sufficiently sorely tried, the problem was nevertheless greatly simplified by the very attitude of such as invoked " French loyalty " to defy the papal commands, without realising—it is their only excuse—the infinite dangers involved in such foolish defiance. Even the national interest was perfectly clear : nothing, at the time, could have done France *greater harm* than to have exposed it, through disobedience to the supreme authority, to a schism between Catholics and to have excited national passions against the spiritual power.

Philosophers should not attempt to evade the *invidiosi veri* mentioned by Dante. They are painful but they must not therefore be left out of consideration. They reveal the extent of the real gravity of the danger of naturalism before referred to ; in such an exceptional case, one so tragically significant as a conflict with the Church, were habits of rash judgement and violence to serve for guide in conduct rather than the virtues of justice and charity ? Was the Church herself to be judged as a natural reality and not as an invisible supernatural reality, the object of theological faith ? Was national interest (identified with the views of one political party) to be taken as the supreme practical rule for the appreciation of things, even of such things as involved religion and the spiritual? Was political empiricism to be absolute and no account taken of the essential subordination of the political good itself to God and Christ and the Church of Christ? The facts themselves gave the answer. It all showed how those who, unconsciously reviving old Jansenist difficulties, profess to obey only if they can give the interior adhesion of their speculative minds to the reasons dictating the orders received—do in fact happen to give such an adhesion of mind. If a certain naturalist appreciation of things is, in various degrees, the common fault of a great many Christians to-day, such a fault is a great deal more pernicious when it affects, as the event has shown only too clearly, the very spirit of a party endowed with such a vigorous and obstinate moral and intellectual personality as the Action Française and is accompanied by a stubborn indocility in regard to the Church. There are sore trials which men may dread because of some particular good which they pursue and they may even seek to avert them, although they must nevertheless acknowledge them to be justified. *Justificata in semetipsa.* The further time removes men's minds from the contingent circumstances surrounding the condemnation and every subsidiary consideration, so that they may be able to consider it in its substance and pure intrinsic reasons, as is only fair, the more apparent will such justice become. It will then be realised that it was not exterior and practical obedience only but the conformity of the speculative judgement also to the pontifical decisions considered in themselves which here answered to the truth of things. It will also be realised how the evils indicated could have been remedied. It must not be forgotten that the severe warnings were transformed into a formal prohibition of the newspaper only because of the latter's practical attitude and *non-filial* resistance. Rome insists upon submission, but is ever careful not to close the door on the possibility of pacification. In any event nobody was required to sacrifice the least of any cherished truths ; all that was required of him was to reject errors and defects and to re-establish all things in the high light of faith.

Writers whose minds are swift to take alarm and appear to be very easily shocked indeed are apprehensive, they say, of a divorce between the Church and the mind [86]. This refrain has often been heard before, more especially when liberalism and modernism were the fashion. And to no purpose, for the spirit knows its own country. At the time of the *Syllabus*, a host of intelligent people, that is to say considering themselves to be such, condemned the Pope's condemnations and opined that, by opposing " progressive forces " which the Church ought to have conciliated, he was leading religion to ruin. Time has passed and the justice and opportunity of Pius IX's action become only the more apparent with every passing day [87].

" Every deliberate deed goes either to the right or the left, to the side of good and God or to the side of evil, just as on the mountain top, where the watershed is, every drop of water goes to the right or the left towards opposite rivers and seas.

" In the spiritual sphere, the watershed is known

61

above all by those who have received the gift of discerning spirits, by the supreme pastor in particular, whose task it is to be a guide to souls in the way of salvation. It is for him, more than anyone, to discern good grain from chaff, to preserve everything worth preserving and make all things work together for the supernatural good of such as seek God in the sincerity of their hearts and are truly desirous of loving Him above all things " [88].

19. There is every indication that we are faced with a grave religious crisis which has not yet ceased to agitate men's minds. On the one hand, the school of thought which now stands condemned appeared to have taken deep root in important areas of French Catholicism ; it had enlisted much sympathy among the clergy and even constituted in many places one of the strongest bulwarks for the defence of religion. On the other hand, by one of those numerous paradoxes to be observed in the state of contemporary France, paradoxes which never cease to surprise even such observers as are most familiar with the intrinsic value of ideas and movements, the Action Française, although not a single one of its members was in Parliament, influenced many minds with the prestige of a quasi-public authority and led opinion. It is now to be feared that certain milieux whose Catholicism was more of a fighting force than an inner life may be affected with a mistrust of spiritual authority and that a redistribution of political forces may ensue which will facilitate an anti-clerical offensive. Should they then have to suffer, Catholics will at any rate realise that nobody will be able to confuse their cause with that of

any political party and their testimony to the Faith will be free of any human alloy.

Such is the first and most proximate benefit which will emerge from the crisis ; the absolute refusal opposed by the Church to whatever would enfeoff religion to a political party of whatever sort appears more clearly than ever.

The temptation to link religion to some political party " of the left " is considerable for men eager to secure positive results (to secure them with unreasonable precipitation), because the evils and injustices of the prevailing social system, against which the spirit of the Gospel inclines us to fight, are also the—at any rate most apparent—object of the protests in which the tendencies " of the left " find their *raison d'être*. The temptation to link religion to some political party " of the right " is considerable for men of principles (when their principles are not sufficiently exalted), especially in times of disorder, because such parties are then as it were the memory of, and the permanent claim to restore, a state of public order which has disappeared. It is also important to realise fully that if it is just and required by the law of God that there be union and collaboration between the Church and the public authority which is the incarnation, so to speak, of the common good of the nation, such a privilege ceases to exist for the partisans of the political ideal of that same authority when, as a result of some upheaval or other, it has fallen from power ; it is then no longer the head of the social body invested with the right of government by the author of nature and representing the common good of all ; it is merely one party among others in the political life of the country. Whatever

63

qualifications it may possess in the order of political rivalries, it has no special right to claim that it is the ally of the Church ; it is even absurd to suppose that what is by definition *universal*, that is to say Catholic, can ever possibly be linked to what is by definition *particular*, that is to say, to a party.

The Church, whose wisdom unites in a superior and *metapolitical* unity all the truths whose temporal application in the sphere of the terrestrial State men must seek politically both " right " and " left," is therefore obliged to combat vigilantly temptations, to which either party may be liable, to enfeoff her to its own policy.[1]

---

[1] " Being also not only a perfect society, but a society superior to every human society, the Church absolutely refuses, by right and duty, to become the slave of any political party and to conform to the shifting exigencies of politics. . . .

" To seek to implicate the Church in such party quarrels and claim to use her support the more easily to triumph over one's opponents is an improper abuse of religion " (Leo XIII, Encyclical *Sapientiae Christianae*).

" Its Catholicism (i.e. of the Sillon)," wrote Pius X, " adapts itself only to the form of democratic government which it considers most favourable to the Church and to be, so to speak, one and the same with the Church ; it therefore enfeoffs its religion to a political party. We need not point out that the advent of universal democracy does not concern the action of the Church in the world, we have already recalled that the Church has always left the nations the care of adopting the government they consider most apt to serve their interests. What we do desire to state once again, following Our Predecessor, is that it is both erroneous and dangerous in principle to enfeoff Catholicism to any particular form of government and that the error and danger are the greater when religion is synthesised with a kind of democracy whose doctrines are erroneous. Such is the case of the Sillon which, compromising the Church in fact, and in favour of a particular form of politics, sows division among Catholics, tears young men and even priests and seminarists away from purely Catholic action and wastefully squanders the living energies of a part of the nation. . . ."

" The leaders of the Sillon," wrote Pius X again, " allege that they are developing their action in a sphere which is not that of the Church, that they pursue only temporal and not spiritual interests, that a Sillonist is merely a Catholic devoted to the cause of the working classes " (Pius X, Letter on the Sillon, 25th August, 1910).

The Church is militant here on earth, but knows that she belongs to Heaven. However strenuously she might unceasingly protest her independence of parties both " right " and " left," the terribly general tendency of the Conservative world to link the defence of its material interests to the defence of religion, so concealing the efforts of Catholics in other spheres, gave rise in many minds to a formidable misunderstanding in this connection. The Action Française affair, by dispelling this misunderstanding, acquires a peculiarly striking symbolic value.

The religious crisis which it seems to inaugurate may be severe : it will be none the less salutary, if only French Catholics have the sense to profit by it and realise the full import of the lesson which, without the slightest doubt, transcends the incident which occasioned it. It is a crisis of liberation, of deliverance. The spiritual must free itself from the earthly fetters which threatened to enslave it. We must realise that, however important human and political means may be in the sphere of the temporal good, they are the least effective for the extension of the kingdom of God and that in proportion as the world falls to pieces they will appear more and more inadequate in that sphere. We must realise that, however necessary any kind of political activity may be, it is confined to a human and particular plane, where religion can make an authoritative intervention for the protection of the spiritual good but can never surrender its own independence.

If Catholics are required, *as Catholics*, to stand outside and above every political party of whatever sort, it goes without saying that, *as citizens*, they can still give their adhesion to any political party they may consider

F   65

useful to the common good, once the Church has not condemned it either for doctrinal errors or dangers of spiritual deviation. The distinction, however, must be properly grasped. Catholics do not then surrender their intellectual and religious preoccupations—how could they leave these out of account in considering the common good ? Their adhesion to any particular political party is a moral choice which remains subordinate to their destination to the ultimate end and their appreciation of spiritual values. But it is directly ordered to the service of the terrestrial State in its subordination to the eternal good, not to the service of the Church itself. And this personal choice of theirs, *as Catholic members of the terrestrial State*, not *as members of the Catholic State*, in no way pledges the Church and affirms no necessity of means linking the fate of Catholicism to any human party, for different minds, animated by the same desire to serve Christ and the Church, may very well form different judgements with regard to the common temporal good, even when it is subordinated, as it ought to be, to eternal interests, and so elect for opposite political parties.

20. The condemnation of the Action Française clearly in no way affects Catholics who, in their search for the good of the terrestrial State, consider that the restoration of monarchy or a policy " of the right " is the best means of securing it. In practice, however, they are in a painful situation, because the party to which they belonged, finding itself unable to conform to the requirements of the Church, withdrew its obedience. Hence a more or less lengthy period of weakness and confusion, the issue of which it is no

business of mine to anticipate (however ardently I may desire some peaceful solution), for the sphere of practical politics is outside the scope of this essay.

If the political situation, however, consequent upon the condemnation of the Action Française is outside the competence of a philosopher, the state of minds does interest and concern him. One thing is immediately apparent from this point of view. The readjustment must be made by working in the deep and the first necessity is a sort of intellectual and moral examination of conscience.

It is clear that in condemning whatever errors and aberrations she perceives in any doctrine or movement, the Church has no intention of condemning whatever good they may contain. Whatever is right and well-founded in political conceptions which, empirically and partially rediscovered by Maurras, go back to Joseph de Maistre, Bonald, Bossuet and St. Thomas Aquinas, remains intact. For minds which now consider as utterly exploded the old revolutionary ideology, the religion of necessary progress and every Rousseauist myth which the world took for the substance of life—the myths of natural Goodness, of democratism,[1] of the General Will and Law as the expression of numbers, of the Liberty of everyone as more important than truth and justice, of the State as the unmoral purveyor of material well-being and lay sovereign, absolute and unlimited, of the Nation or Humanity as the incarnation of an immanent God, etc.—there can be no ques-

[1] That is to say of the people as perpetual possessor and sole lawful possessor of sovereignty. (Cf. Appendix IV and the author's *Three Reformers*, ch. iii.)

tion of going back, of making any concession whatever to such false and essentially obsolete ideas. There must be a progress still further forward and higher up in the movement, leaving them far behind. The only salvation is in the whole truth. A Christian policy cannot maintain itself without its philosophical and theological principles, must have a complete conception of political reality itself, with all the moral values, relations of justice and responsibilities in the order of the family no less than of society which such a conception implies and whose source is truly religious ; it must realise that the false liberal dogmas, so effectively combated by Maurras on the plane of immediate experience, consist in denying not only the subjection of the individual to the political whole, but also and in the first place, the subjection of man to God in the natural and the supernatural order, according to Cajetan's great expression which seems to summarise in anticipation the whole doctrine of Leo XIII on liberalism : " Whether it be in relation to natural happiness, either private or political, or to supernatural happiness, man is always subject (to some superior authority) " [89] ; in a word and figuratively speaking, a Christian policy must select its historical *analogue*,[1] not in the century of Louis XIV, when so much pride of life ran to seed amid such brilliance, but in the theological civilisation of the Middle Ages. On this condition only will it be possible to pass beyond the sphere in which another naturalism may take the place of the naturalism of freedom of a Spinoza, a Rousseau

---

[1] An *analogy* and nothing but an *analogy* is here intended. Time, we know, is irreversible. It is a question of spiritual correspondence, not of literal copy. It is not a question of a material return to the Middle Ages, but of drawing inspiration from their principles.

or a Kant, the naturalism of authority of a Hobbes or a Mandeville.[1]

Many of those who, by a process of abstraction, retained of the Action Francaise movement almost exclusively the spiritual renovations carried out by Maurras in the sphere of political thought, hoped that the great intellectual activity he stimulated would be gradually exalted and transfigured under the influence of grace, so that by a kind of organic evolution, the imperfect and as it were vegetative form of pure empiricism might in the end give way to the spiritual soul of metaphysics and theology. Such hope events have shown to have been based upon too optimistic a judgement.

The fact nevertheless remains that, even at the risk of a very painful crisis and although such things were at first understood only by a few, the truths acknowledged by the criticism of liberal and revolutionary ideology must be delivered in a higher synthesis than the mere nationalist idea could ever guarantee. The word was invented in France to meet a historical situation of a very peculiar sort, in circumstances and amid dangers of a particularly local and momentary kind, and won many adherents. At the present day the most adequate expression of the profound aspirations of the human being in his struggles against death is to be found not only in the word *nationalism* [90], but also and in the first place in the word *universalism*. There is no other authentic and truly supranational universalism than Catholicism The minds of men can only re-adjust themselves to the present needs of the world by adjusting themselves to the Catholic

[1] Cf. Appendix VI.

absolute. As their view so becomes more elevated, so also its horizon expands.

Men in our time are summoned to an integral restoration of Christian values, to a universal reinvention of order. They must expel from their minds all the barbarism, both capitalist and communist, of the naturalist and atheist world ; not only in the political sphere, but also in the economic and social sphere which has been corrupted by the system of the fertility of money, and in the sphere of international relations and—most important of all—in the sphere of intellectual and religious life. There can be no true and complete order in human life unless grace and charity are predominant, for every practical order presupposes that the will is in direct relation to its ends and therefore the pre-eminence of the love of the supreme Good. If peace is *the work of justice*[1] and if charity presupposes justice, nevertheless—it is a fundamental law of the State and life—" True and authentic peace depends on charity still more than on justice ; the function of justice is to remove the obstacles in the way of peace, such as acts of injustice and injuries, peace being peculiarly and particularly charity in operation."[2] This is the confused feeling of everyone to-day. But if the desired union of hearts is not realised in theological charity which consists in loving with one same love

[1] Isaias xxxii. 17.
[2] Encyclical *Ubi Arcano Dei*. Pius XI is here recalling, as he explicitly indicates a few lines earlier, the following passage from St. Thomas : " Peace is the work of justice *indirectly*, so far, that is to say, as it removes a hindrance. But it is the work of charity *directly* : because charity begets peace of its own nature : for love is a unifying force (*vis unitiva*), as Dionysius says (*De divin. nomin*, ch. iv, lect. xii): but peace is a union of the appetitive inclinations." *Sum. Theol.*, ii–ii, 29, 3, ad 3.

God for His own sake and man for God's sake, the disillusion will be bitter. Such genuine love has its roots in faith, and faith presupposes reason. Catholicism alone—and of all its doctors the *common Doctor of the Church*—makes man understand that the absolute primacy of charity, so far from being opposed to reason, rather presupposes it : that reason still remains " the first principle of human actions," [1] but as implying in the appetite unswerving devotion to the last end and as itself illumined by faith and the infused gifts. We must make no mistake. The action of the Church in the past twenty-five years appears as a vigilant, unwearying defence of charity itself, which is the life of her life and the eternal justification for her existence ; the Church defends it in the hearts of her children both against the influence of hatred and against the influence of false love ; against the hardening caused by the naturalist worship of the race or the nation and the deliquescence caused by the naturalist worship of humanity and the modernist corruption of reason and faith ; for theological faith is the source of all supernatural life and the divine love. In truth the order to which we tend has intelligence for its foundation and charity for its end : we see it simultaneously suspended from supernatural love and supported upon baptised reason.

As far as France is concerned, it is important to remember all the fidelity to grace its vocation implies, the wealth of consecrated property invested in the patrimony and destiny of a Christian nation. The salvation of a Christian nation is not a casual operation: it necessitates the acknowledgement of the super-

[1] St. Thomas Aquinas, *Sum. Theol.*, i–ii, 58, 2.

natural order and the employment of proportioned means, elevated in the use to which they are put by the virtues from above. For the means must be proportioned to the end, a very simple axiom neglected nowadays by many who seek in the most intense natural activity the means of attaining an end involving the supernatural order. God is the leader of history ; the common task is merely to prepare the way, each of us doing his duty to the best of his ability, in the first place by raising his mind and heart to the height of the whole truth.

II. JOAN OF ARC OR PHILIP THE FAIR

21. Preaching obedience does not make for popularity. It is a doctrine poor in demagogic values, distasteful to all men. The French national temperament, moreover, is quick to take offence, passionately devoted to liberty, prone to contradict and besides particularly exacting as regards authority in the matter of psychological discernment. Obedience then, you would say, is difficult for Frenchmen. In reality, however, the French love to obey, if only they are told why ; the fidelity which is at the heart of obedience has a great attraction for them and their rebellions, as often as not, are mere outbursts of impatience at not being ordered enough. May one be permitted to quote the Gospel, adapting it ? " A certain man had two sons, and coming to the first, he said : ' Son, go work to-day in my vineyard.' And he answering said : ' I will not.' But afterwards, being moved by repentance, he went. And coming to the other, he said in like manner. And he answering,

said : ' I go, sir,' and he went not ; which of the two did the father's will ? " [1] The Frenchman, to be sure.

Two opposite traditions cross and mingle throughout the course of French history, the sacred and the profane ; one really made France, the other by striving to elevate it according to the ambitions of the flesh, prepared the way for the forces which tended to undo it ; the first was predominant in the Middle Ages and informed the admirable limited monarchy (*regimen mixtum*) [91], elaborated by bishops and kings ; it found its purest manifestation in St. Louis and in Joan of Arc its immaculate angel of sorrows. The second remains situate under the sign of Philip the Fair, grew up with absolute monarchy, tainted the policy of Richelieu (who was far from vexed to see the formulation of the theory of the *State Catholic*) [92], and flourished in the *Gallican liberties vis-à-vis* the Pope (that is to say *Gallican servilities vis-à-vis* the King). Such a naturalist conception of patriotism was the chief fault of the *ancien régime*.[2] If it was to be found in men who in other respects were devoted servants of the country, we should not forget what a deadly burden its consequences in home and foreign politics, more particularly the protection accorded to the Protestant princes and Prussia, imposed upon the future of France in return for proximate and palpable glowing advantages. A baptised nation *can not* ensure its greatness upon principles opposed to the laws of the Gospel or by sacrificing the common interests of the Christian commonwealth. The result of so doing for France and the world (for such a sin, far from being peculiar

[1] Matthew xxi. 28-31.   [2] Cf. Appendix VII.

to France, has been as serious, even more serious elsewhere and is indeed the common fate of the whole modern world) proceeded from an inexorable logic. It has often been observed that the same principles of *rebellion of the part against the whole* which were made to serve against the Pope necessarily did duty against the kings and then against the country itself. Nogaret is first cousin to Robespierre and Lenin. The refusal to submit to the Church necessarily involved a corollary refusal to submit to God and to admit His rights over the State as such. The regalian decrees of the Parliaments are the rough draft of the lay laws.

Histories of France, conservative and radical alike, all stand in need of drastic revision from this point of view. The homicidal ideas informing the world which issued from the Reformation and the Revolution, perverting therein normal developments which pursue their course elsewhere, are the *cadaverous forms* of the corruption of the Christian world, progressively destroyed by the claim of modern politicians and philosophers, kings and nations, to absolute independence (*aseity*). It was five hundred years ago that we began to die.

It seems useless to repeat such an experiment. The restoration of order will be wholly Christian or an utter failure.

" The realm does not belong to the Dauphin, but to God," said Joan of Arc to Baudricourt in 1429, " and yet it is God's will that the Dauphin be crowned king and hold his realm *in commendam*." She had no doubt of the royal right of the Dauphin before leading him to Rheims but until then she refused to call him king ; for it was from the Consecration that there dated for

74

Joan "not the political legitimacy of Charles VII, but his supernatural legitimacy, so to speak, the perfect exercise of his vice-gerency over the land of France in the name of Jesus Christ" [93]. The Consecration which Joan so ardently desired is itself an act of homage to the spiritual suzerainty of the Church ; it is the most striking sign, impressed upon the crown itself, of the rights of the spiritual power over political things, so far as these affect the welfare of souls. Consider Joan of Arc at Rheims clasping the knees of the king : " Now is the pleasure of God fulfilled, Who desired that I should raise the siege of Orleans and lead you to this city of Rheims to receive your worthy Consecration, proving you to be true king. . . ." The king, thenceforth, shares in the ministry of the Church—*per hanc (coronam) te participem ministerii nostri non ignores* [1]—and in virtue thereof rules. Joan would have him spend himself in the restoration of Christendom : she saw him riding with the English at the head of a new crusade. . . .

A century and a quarter earlier, there was a king of France who turned against the Church the authority she had consecrated. By the sacrilegious hand of Guillaume de Nogaret, Philip the Fair seized and imprisoned and outraged the Pope at Anagni. Seated on his throne, with the tiara on his head and the keys and the cross in his hands, the great old man, Boniface VIII, in whom the Middle Ages had taken refuge, waited for the coming of the men of blood. " Inasmuch as I am betrayed like Jesus Christ, I will at any rate die like a Pope." He died, indeed, some days later, of grief. So the " little boy "—*nos deponeremus regem ita*

[1] Formula of the *Roman Pontifical*.

sicut unum garcionem—intimated his majority to the world and that with the assistance of his lawyers he was preparing to inaugurate the modern policy of national self-seeking. That the Church had any right to intervene in matters of State, even for the defence of ecclesiastical immunities, was for the first time officially denied by the eldest daughter of the Church. I note that, while proceeding to the extreme limits of outrage against the Papacy, while shamefully calumniating Boniface VIII, forging his bulls and describing the Vicar of Christ as a " malefactor " and "infamous bandit " [94], Philip the Fair and his friends professed themselves the best Catholics in the world and the most devoted sons of the Church, but " subject, themselves, their people and their followers, to the protection of our Holy Mother the Church, the Council and others to whom it should belong, *only in regard to the spiritual* " [95], that is to say, provided always that the spiritual allowed the temporal and the *summa regis libertas* to do as they pleased in the world. There was as it were the first *separation* of the Roman Church and the French State or more generally, and in the language of Kant, of " morality " and " law." They added, also, " that the King has been empowered by God to defend and exalt the faith and that prelates are invited thereto *in partem sollicitudinis.*" And the prelates, who signed whatever the king wanted, accepted that point of view. So that in reality, as in every similar case, the claim for the absolute independence of the temporal was converted into an attempt to subordinate the spiritual to the temporal ; the whole commotion excited in the kingdom by the lawyers of Philip the Fair was a prearranged and perfectly organised movement, " with the sole object of setting the Pope aside, absorbing the episcopate and placing the entire Church in the hands of the civil power." Such is the conclusion arrived at by the latest historian of the conflict.[1]

The true heirs of Philip the Fair are the anti-clerical and laicising radicals ; the monarchists of the school of the Count de Chambord had, it was believed, freed themselves from such a spirit. But the two traditions mentioned were mingled in the nationalist movement, although many had hoped that the sacred tradition would ultimately prevail amongst men who had fought so courageously for public honour to be paid to Joan of Arc.

The significance of the present crisis will be better understood, if it is borne in mind that before first warning and then condemning the Action Française, Pius XI solemnly condemned laicism and as solemnly proclaimed the universal kingship of Christ.[2]

A divine intention appears through the mist of human history : Catholics who devote their energies to the reconstruction of France must take their choice among the principles of the national tradition and explicitly reject those which cannot but be considered as the primary root of the evils afflicting their country. Providence is now challenging them to choose between the spirit of Philip the Fair and the spirit of Joan of Arc. The spiritual event taking place to-day in each of them, in the intimacy of their liberty, is much more important for the history of the future than many visible changes.

[1] Jean Rivière, *Le problème de l'Église et de l'État au temps de Philippe le Bel*, 1926, p. 118.
[2] The Encyclicals *Ubi Arcano Dei* and *Quas Primas*.

OUR FIRST DUTY TO GOD

I. SUPREMACY OF THE CHURCH

22. THE moral of the crisis which confronts us is self-evident ; it is a reminder of the exigencies of the supernatural life, an absolute affirmation of the primacy of the spiritual.

Such a primacy presents itself to us under three different aspects which the doctrine of St. Thomas, better than any other after the Gospel and St. Paul, enables us to understand. Does not St. Thomas himself constantly preach the primacy of the spirit by precept and example ? By his general teaching with regard to Christ and the Redemption, as by his observations on civil government and the Church, he shows us the supremacy of the Church in all its force.

By his doctrine concerning nature and grace and the subordination of ends, he makes us understand the primacy of spiritual over political ends, and of the universal domain of grace over all the particular divisions of nature.

By his doctrine concerning human life and the virtues, he reveals the primacy of infused contemplation, peculiar to minds raised by grace to a share of the divine life, over the exterior activity which is common (by analogy) to bodies and minds.

23. We must assert as a truth superior to every vicissitude of time the supremacy of the Church over the world and all earthly powers. If the universe is not to suffer a radical disorder, the Church must lead the nations to the ultimate end of human life, which is also that of States, and must therefore, in virtue of the spiritual interests entrusted to her, direct governments and nations and bend before God the stiff necks of the powers of flesh. On that condition only will they be stable : " For He does not take away mortal kingdoms Who gives the kingdom of Heaven : He confirms them." [1] The Pope is living Authority. On the summit of humanity, we see in him the imprint of the face of Christ. If that authority is not obeyed by Christian nations, what authority will hold ? The economy of the world is breaking up. And if that authority is obeyed, it inspires the hearts of men with the spirit of love which constitutes unity.

The great convulsions of the modern world are memories of the unity which has been lost. It is metaphysically impossible for it to recover peace without justice, that is to say, in the first place, without the submission which is owing to God [96]—and unity, without the principle of unity on this earth, that is to say, without the effective acknowledgement of the supremacy of the spiritual power. Men may listen to the truth or they may not, the truth must still be told. The Papacy has been telling the truth for years with an energy which has never flagged.

It was for the good of nations and States, not for her own good, that the Church once helped them to

[1] Hymn *Crudelis Herodes* in the Office of the Epiphany, quoted by Pope Pius XI in the Encyclical *Quas Primas*, 11th December, 1925.

do their temporal work in such a way as suited the requirements of the supernatural end. The apostasy of the nations is exerting itself to relieve the Church more and more from any such anxiety. We should be under no mistake as to what such an apostasy means to the world. What sort of benefit did it formerly receive from the order which subjected it more or less effectively to the Church and her spiritual laws ? The Church did not make the world holy or just : the world remained the world. She did not make it comfortable or restful or agreeable : the world remained a vale of tears. She made it *habitable*. The mass of men could fulfil their destiny on earth in the common conditions of human life without being obliged to heroism. If the Saints had themselves crucified with Christ, it was for love, not of necessity. Nowadays the devil has made such a mess of everything in the system of life on earth that the world will presently become uninhabitable for anybody but Saints. The rest will drag their lives out in despair or fall below the level of man. The antinomies of human life are too exasperated, the burden of matter too oppressive ; merely to exist, one has to expose oneself to too many snares. Christian heroism will one day become the sole solution for the problems of life. Then, as God proportions His graces to human needs and tempts nobody beyond his strength, we shall doubtless see coincident with the worst condition in human history a flowering of sanctity. . . .

24. If we consider at all attentively the state of apostasy of the modern world, we shall not be surprised that, while not denying the urgency of a return

to sound political ideas or the right of Catholics, like
any others, to strive to secure by every honourable
means the triumph of the political system they think
best suited to their country or the importance of the
civil and political duties imposed on each of us by
the fourth commandment, the Church nowadays
not only insists, as she has always done, upon her
indifference with regard to the various forms of lawful
government, but also herself adopts an attitude
more and more *apolitical* or rather *supra-political*. She
has no longer to exercise her spiritual authority
among the nations, as in the Christian centuries,
to direct governments positively towards religious
ends, but must henceforth in the first place defend
her rights and the liberties of her children against
aggression and prevent religion becoming too closely
implicated in political struggles. She therefore
approves of Catholics exercising whatever political
activity they prefer, provided such activity does not
tend to diminish or pervert in them the spirit of the
Gospel. She admits that on this condition they may
collaborate with infidels. She will not have Catholic
influence and action *as such* bound to any party, any
class, any political servitude.[1]

With regard to the very reserved attitude of the
Holy See towards fascism and its strictures upon the
Action Française, certain persons, forming an impertinent judgement on matters pertaining to the Church,
have spoken of a " sliding to the left " ; as though
what is built upon a rock could slide to right or left.
We are in reality summoned to an affirmation of
supernatural faith, to a strenuous asseveration of the

[1] Cf. p. 64.

rights of the spiritual against the most powerful political and temporal enterprises, even against such as proffer their support. For the Church fears the protection of a human arm which is not in the first place absolutely docile to God (and the docility of whatever is powerful, while it has always been rare, in the modern world is almost a miracle). It is the great principles of spiritual independence and sovereignty which modern liberalism most detests, and of which St. Gregory VII was the supreme incarnation, which are here in issue.

The Church makes her way amidst dangers springing from the most opposite quarters to imperil the souls of men, striking at one time to one side, at another time to another. Anyone with his eyes fixed on the present thinks that she is changing direction every time ; it is the danger which changes direction, the Church marches straight on. She repudiates none, rescinds none, renounces none of her decisions. The encyclical *Pascendi* is still there, the *Syllabus* is still there, the Bull *Unam Sanctam* is still there. Liberalism still stands condemned, Americanism, Socialism, Sillonism, Modernism still stand condemned. Laicism is still and again condemned.[1] If we consider, as we ought, the prodigious *memory* of the Church and the eternal perspectives where she insists we shall take our stand to contemplate her actions, we shall then see the solemn proclamation of the kingship of Christ related in the closest connection throughout the centuries with the resounding affirmations of the supremacy of the spiritual made by the Popes of the Middle Ages and that the present attitude of the

[1] Cf. the encyclicals *Ubi Arcano* and *Quas Primas*.

Church in regard to nationalism, even such nationalism as is most anxious to rely on the Catholic tradition, is dictated by the great memories in which they all continue to live who rose up like " a rampart for the house of Israel : Paschal II against the Emperor Henry IV ; Innocent IV against Frederick II ; Boniface VIII against Philip the Fair ; Gregory XIII, Sixtus V, Gregory XIV and Clement VIII against Henry of Bourbon ; Innocent XI against Louis XIV ; Clement XIII against the courts of Madrid, Lisbon, Naples and Parma ; Pius VII against Napoleon ; Gregory XVI against Frederick William . . ." [97]. She has a longer memory than any of us, the experience of all history. It is folly to reject the advice of such wisdom or to be concerned at the course she may be taking.

But it is folly no less to betray her designs and to rush out, as though that were the way indicated by her, to embrace errors she has ever rebuked. If Catholics think that they are entering into the mind of the Pope by compounding with the spirit of " modern liberties " condemned by the Pope, by abandoning the eternal rules of doctrine or by savouring the sweetness of accommodating their baptised souls to the concupiscences of the age in the hope of a return to the age of innocence through the virtues of evolution and human progress, they will suffer a cruel awakening.

It is important also not to forget that if the Church herself is essentially supra-political, every Catholic, on the other hand, considered as a member of the terrestrial community, is in the State and of the State, not above it, and must contribute his share of work for the temporal salvation of the State and the world.

Certain political conditions, subordinate though they may be to spiritual conditions, are indispensable to such temporal salvation. The Church, which pursues another end—an eternal end—has never failed to acknowledge, would even sanctify such conditions of temporal good and by the very fact of ordering them to the ultimate supernatural end guarantees from above their integrity.

II. PRIMACY OF THE SPIRITUAL

25. We should be sorry for Churches which are separated from the Pope ; they have nobody to defend them against the power of the world. There is no man raised above all the kings to interpose his hand and the hand of God between them and the instinct of tyranny natural to the civil power. The Russian Church had never *accepted*, as is too commonly thought in the West, the oppression she suffered at the hands of the Imperial Government ; she prayed in secret for her liberty : Lenin and martyrdom were required to set her free—in a terrible persecution. But is her freedom genuine and permanent ?

We should be sorry also for nations that know not the Church and the Pope. They cannot adjust the spiritual and the temporal in a proper harmony. If the temporal authority does not become a usurping power—the general rule—the spiritual authority absorbs the temporal and reigns like a despot as in Tibet. Attempts at ordinary subordination succeed only in confusing everything ; a deep-seated presentiment of the primacy of the spirit impelled the like of Gandhi to make war on the British by fasting and penances and suffering deliberately chosen ; but that is to require heroism of the multitude and it is to be feared that such a direct application of spiritual methods to a domain which is specifically temporal—civic and national—may end in streams of blood.

The example of Gandhi, however, should put us to shame. It is everywhere forgotten in Europe, which once was Christian, that if specifically political means ought to be applied to specifically political ends, nevertheless, by the very fact of their proximate end being subordinated to a more exalted end, the use of such means ought itself to be rectified and elevated by more exalted virtues and impregnated as it were by their spirit. Only on that condition are they completely good and effective *in their order* ; for only in that case are they perfectly subject to the whole order of their ends. Joan of Arc would have had her army in a state of grace before waging battle ; every method of hers was loyal and pure ; by her solemn warnings the rights of charity were maintained even in regard to enemies. States nowadays have turned their methods of existence into an organised system of sin.

The truth is that Europe has forgotten even the subordination of political to spiritual ends. There lies its great mistake. Hence derive that general condition of the oppression of the spirit and the conscience, that contempt in practice for human personality and its dignity, the overwhelming burden of which is everywhere more or less consciously felt. We should be sorry above all for nations which, gathered by a signal favour of grace around the Pope and having in their midst the voice of Christ indefatigably reminding them of all that Truth requires, have persisted for centuries in stopping up their ears. *Generatio incredula et perversa, usque quo patiar vos ?* [1]

26. It would appear that we are on the threshold of an age when, all the high hopes set upon nationalism and humanitarian optimism having been disappointed, the great problems of the spiritual order, the war between the angels, will once more dominate history and the distress of mankind. This is what the Russian philosopher, Nicholas Berdiaeff, calls a new Middle Age. It is most striking to consider from this point of view the ferment at work within the Church. All her aspirations at the moment seem to be strained towards a spiritual restoration of Christendom. The spirit of God is making her cry out with her whole heart in the hope of that holy task. We should be sorry for anyone who judged a movement of such divine origin according to the standards of politics, national conflicts and worldly interests. Jesus Christ is moving His chalice from one place to another throughout the world, extending the frontiers of the Church, augmenting everywhere within her labour and desire in distant preparation for the return of the Christian East to unity, or the end of the fratricidal schisms provoked by the Reformation, or imploring Heaven to make the scales fall from the eyes of the elder race, or extending the secular effort of the missions and solemnly inviting the nations of Asia to share in the plenitude of the priesthood and the government of churches.[2]

[1] Matthew xvii. 16.

[2] The encyclicals of the Supreme Pontiffs are a testimony as it were in every age to the action of the Holy Ghost. Nothing is more significant at the present day than the whole of the encyclicals and

This is an essentially *spiritual* work which is being accomplished ; the affirmation of unity and Catholicity necessitated not only by the rents caused by the war, but also, it would appear, by a presentiment of the future. The universal supplications of Good Friday are heard above the din and clamour of the age . . . as though the Church were gathering all her love together in preparation for some divine work before the great anguish.

We should strive to the utmost to bring that spiritual Christendom down into the arena of the temporal and to realise it in political Christendom ; may it be considered probable at present ? A Christian political order in the world is not to be artificially constructed by diplomatic means ; it is a product of the spirit of faith. It presupposes a living practical faith in the majority, a civilisation with the impress of theology and the acknowledgement of all the rights of God in the life of the State. We are far from such an ideal. Unless God intervenes miraculously or excess of despair compels this distracted world to a moment's obedience, the kingdoms of earth seem destined for long to the most deadly divisions.

It is understandable that when nations are in a state so far removed from real order and even the most precarious peace is so difficult to secure, countries, especially those whose frontiers are most exposed, should refuse to abandon the precautions in arma-

decrees of Pius XI (more particularly the encyclical *Ubi Arcano Dei* on securing the Peace of Christ through the kingdom of Christ, *Quas Primas* on the Kingship of Christ, *Rerum Ecclesiae* on missions and a native clergy, *Studiorum Ducem* on St. Thomas Aquinas, *Ecclesiam Dei* on St. Josaphat). An interesting number of the *Revue des Jeunes* (15th March, 1926) contains a collection of articles on these encyclicals.

ments upon which their existence depends. As Catholics in the different countries are as a rule and very normally the element most devoted to the principles of the natural law, it is also understandable that from this point of view they should be conscious, as citizens, of specially grave duties and be the first to require from their governments all the strength of action and preparation necessary for the protection of their native land. Such is indeed the most proximate and essential objective which a Christian policy ought to set before itself.

It would not be Christian, however, if this proximate end were not related to a more remote and exalted end in such a way that the idea of the good of the human community, founded on justice and charity, and of a permanent peace to be established among the nations not merely enjoyed a primacy of honour over such a policy, but actually exercised an effectively controlling action. The sense of obligation towards the country in which we are born and brought up is, like the sense of obligation to parents, a virtue related to justice ; we are indebted to our country for benefits of every kind which we have received from her and they are innumerable. " After God, it is to his parents and his country that a man owes most." [1] But patriot-

---

[1] St. Thomas Aquinas, *Sum. Theol.*, ii–ii, 101, 1. "A man is constituted a debtor to others in a variety of ways, according to their various degrees of excellence and the various benefits he has received from them ; in both cases, however, God occupies the highest place, for God is the supreme degree of excellence and the first principle of our being and government. Our parents and our country are, secondarily, the first principles of our being and government through whom and in which we are born and brought up ; therefore, after God, man is most indebted to his parents and his country ; accordingly, as it is a religious act to do reverence to God, so, in the second place, it is a pious act to do reverence to one's parents and one's country."

sal State in which our nature will be self-sufficient, like the angelic nature. Now man is a material being : and as the object thus pursued on the material side, which divides, is an absolute self-sufficiency which even the angels lack, a deeper descent becomes obviously necessary down to the spirit itself which had resolved to be self-sufficient ; utopian and humanitarian to begin with, in its preparatory phase of desire, the pursuit of such a unity of man regardless of Christ ends by becoming, in its positive phase of realisation, the pretext for the imposition on man of an absolute violence and an anti-human tyranny.

The other universalism seeks the unity of man from the Father of creatures ; respecting every natural diversity, it raises above the nations the true universal State which is the Church and in which man, by supernatural grace, attains to the freedom of the sons of God. The two universalisms are implacably opposed to one another in irreconcilable antagonism. In one case man would make himself divine by his own energy, in the other he is made divine by the blood of the incarnate God. The former universalism is of the devil, homicidal from the very beginning, head of the Church of evil.[1] The latter is of the Redeemer. Bolshevist imperialism, in its effort to expand throughout the world, would seem to proclaim the time when only the universalism of Antichrist and the universalism of Christ will be left facing each other here on earth.

The latter is called Catholicity. True universalism, let it not be forgotten, is the very reverse of eclecticism.

[1] *Diabolus est caput omnium malorum*, St. Thomas Aquinas. *Sum. Theol.*, iii, 8, 7.

It does not marry the *yea* and the *nay*, Heaven and Hell. It presupposes a *yea*, but a *yea* vast enough to fill earth and sky—and excluding the *nay* for all eternity. The universality of truth and faith, which excludes error, is the indispensable condition of the universality of love, which excludes nothing that exists [101]. Authentic universalism is *centred*. A city is at the centre of the universe and makes its unity. AMOR is the same word as ROMA. To speak less superficially : Christ is the head of all humanity. All men belong to Him, good and bad, faithful and infidel.[1] All are intended to become members of Him, are members of Him *potentially*. " His empire," writes Pius XI, adopting the words of his predecessor Leo XIII, " extends not only to the Catholic nations or to those which, purified by holy baptism, belong of right to the Church, although erroneous opinions may have driven them astray and keep them apart or schism have separated them from charity ; it embraces also all mankind that have no knowledge of the Christian faith, so that in all truth the universality of the human race is subject to the power of Jesus Christ."[2] For this reason the Pope, to whom, as Vicar of Christ, every human creature is subject by necessity of salvation [102], is authorised to offer all mankind to their Creator in his prayer.[3] "Lord be King not only of the faithful who have never left Your side, but also of the prodigals who have abandoned You. . . .

[1] St. Thomas Aquinas, *Sum. Theol.*, iii, 8, 3, ad 1.

[2] Encyclical *Quas Primas*, 11th December, 1928, quoting Pope Leo XIII's encyclical *Annum sacrum*, 25th May, 1899.

[3] Leo XIII put this universal authority into practice when he consecrated the whole human race to the Sacred Heart (encyclical *Annum sacrum*).

Be King of all those who are still astray in the darkness of idolatry and Islamism, and do not refuse to draw them all into the radiance of Your Kingdom. Look with pity upon the children of that people which was once Your chosen people ; may the Blood which of old they called down upon their heads descend upon them also, but now in baptism of life and redemption."[1]

28. Whatever injures Catholicity injures Christ. It is the last hope of the human race.

It would be a deadly error to confuse the universal cause of the Church with the particular cause of a civilisation, to confuse, for example, *Latinism* with *Catholicism*, or *Westernism* with *Catholicism*. Catholicism is not linked to the culture of the West. Universality is not confined to one part of the world.

Christ died for East and West. His Divinity embraces East and West in one same uncreated love. As Man, He was born " a Jew by excellence of nature " in the centre where East meets West.

I am well aware of the dangers to the mind latent in the confused syncretism which decks itself in the colours of the East, and the encounter between the ideology with which Europe poisons the world, and from which we can free ourselves only with difficulty, and the great amorphous demons of the false religions of Asia. That is, however, a common plague, a common peril proceeding not from the East, but from the universalism of the devil contaminating East and West by one another. The swarm of pseudo-Christs is the product of such conjunctions of evil.

[1] Formula of universal consecration to the Sacred Heart, modified by Pius XI on the occasion of the Feast of Christ the King, *Acta Apostolicae Sedis*, 5th November, 1925.

Let us make no mistake : the complaints and curses which the East utters against us at the present day are inspired not only by hatred but also by a profound disillusion. We cannot hear that outcry without quivering for sorrow and shame. What would it be *if they knew the gift of God* which we owed them and which we have kept to abuse it—which our missions sought to convey to them but our vices stopped on the way ? The labour of the missionaries, their charity, the testimony they so often sealed in their blood, are the glory of Europe and perhaps its ransom. But far from helping them as it ought, Europe by its sins has constantly thwarted them. For a century past, it has constituted itself the apostle of its own apostasy.[1] Before becoming indignant with our accusers, let us first admit that we have sinned against them and that the diffusion of our atheistic pseudo-culture and that self-styled scientific modernism, which is a gospel of damnation, has merely succeeded in emptying the world of its living energies and spiritual reserves. The claim put forward by certain representatives of the East to be ambassadors of the spirit reveals an illusion which is far from being innocuous. It also conceals a painful aspiration which only the Church of Jesus Christ can satisfy.

As a Catholic and a member of that universal Church, I expect no message of salvation from Buddhism or Taoism, but I feel myself in the first place accountable to all those men in the mystery of reversibility.

I would take leave to refer to what I had recently occasion to write that " if Mr. Hilaire Belloc means

[1] Cf. Appendix VIII.

that Europe would be nothing without the Faith and that its *raison d'être* has been and remains to dispense the Faith to the world, Mr. Belloc is right in saying that Europe is the Faith. But speaking absolutely, no ! Europe is not the Faith and the Faith is not Europe: Europe is not the Church and the Church is not Europe. Rome is not the capital of the Latin world. Rome is the capital of the world. *Urbs caput orbis.* The Church is universal because she is born of God, all nations are at home in her, the arms of her crucified Master are stretched above all races, above all civilisations. She does not bring nations *the benefits of civilisation*, but the Blood of Christ and supernatural Beatitude. It seems as though some kind of marvellous epiphany of her Catholicity were in preparation in our time, of which the progressive development in missionary countries of a native clergy and a native episcopate may be considered a precursory sign " [103].

Before being combated from without by the false Catholicity of the Adversary, this holy Catholicity has been constantly thwarted from within by the selfishness of man. There is no need to mention the spiritual disasters precipitated in the course of centuries by human rivalries in the Church or the ambitions, commercial cupidity and interested designs of governments. For the honour of Catholicism, a Las Casas was found to denounce at the outset the scandals of which the natives of Central and Southern America were the victims [104], and to throw over them the protection of the justice of Christ [105]. Rapacity, however, proved the stronger. To the methods adopted by English colonists in North America and

India reformed Christianity had no opposition to offer. The history of modern colonisation, heroic in its soldiers but dishonoured by gold, bears a heavy burden of iniquities of which the " opium war " [106] is merely one among many. All that is part of the world's business and will be paid for at a price. What I here wish to emphasise is a fact of the spiritual order. Prejudices regarding the radical inferiority of the non-white races, which affected the minds of clergy and laity alike, and even of many of those who devoted themselves to preaching the gospel, have too long caused missionaries to be considered not as the apostles of Jesus Christ only but of a particular human or national culture also, sometimes even as the fore-runners of colonists and merchants. There lay one of the chief obstacles to the evangelisation of the world. The Church is now doing away with that obstacle. She is reminding us that her missionaries must renounce every worldly interest, every concern with national propaganda, must know nothing but Christ, and that they are sent to found churches which shall be self-sufficient, complete with clergy. She does not profess that all races and nations have the same historical vocation and a similar human develop-ment ; she does maintain, in the most significant manner, that they are all called of God, all alike included in her charity, that each has its legitimate place in the spiritual unity of Christendom and is capable of providing the flock of Christ with bishops. European Christians might take to heart the words recently addressed to the undergraduates of Louvain by one of the Chinese bishops recently consecrated by Pius XI, Dr. Philip Tchao [107] : " Cultivate

amongst you," he told them, " manifest around you,
the sentiments of Catholic fraternity which yesterday
brought tears of joy to our eyes. . . . The hearts of
pagans, like the rest, hunger and thirst for charity.
We Catholics, who are the children of the same Father,
redeemed by the same Jesus, nourished by the same
Eucharist, must break down once and for all race
and colour barriers, national prejudices and anti-
pathies, and loyally love one another with our whole
hearts, with the whole strength of our wills, if need
be. . . . In a world divided by so many misunder-
standings and torn by so many hatreds, on the day
when the infidels will be able to repeat of the Catholics
of all countries the celebrated words spoken about the
early Christians in Rome : *Just see how they love one
another* !—on that day the Church will have conquered
Satan.   For Satan is hatred and Christ is love " [108].

29. It would be foolish to think that, in liberating
itself from old fetters, Catholicity will not find fresh
dangers to meet, against which it must be on its guard.
The nationalism of the young nations in a high fever
of emancipation is as capable of great excesses as the
nationalism of the exhausted nations and States
heavily laden with history ; their susceptibility is no
less quick to take offence ; it is far from certain that the
world which set out to behold a deliverance is not
simply taking part in a change of servitude.

To speak less superficially : it may be observed that
every moment of *deliverance* is for humanity a moment
of danger.   We should always be on our guard against
sudden releases, because our nature is weak and bent
beneath such a heavy load.   At the slightest sensation

H   97

of alleviation, it imagines that all the constraints and all the old misery, all the rigour of the law, are about to cease.

This is the reason why, after the great deliverance of the Cross and the Resurrection and Pentecost, God reserved for it such a long and bitter penance. The persecutions of the early centuries, the anguish and the agonies of the Dark Ages, were the *noli me tangere*, as it were, of the Holy Ghost ; under cover of such darkness He kept Christ and the redemption alive in the souls of men. Oppressed by the constraints not of fear but of love, compelled by suffering to make an avowal of love *and prove it*, as Père de Foucauld said, they did not let their deliverance go the way of the flesh. The Christian centuries needed such a schooling to teach them where to find true liberty.

Yet it was a question then of a genuine and divine deliverance, the only deliverance. The world experienced later another deliverance, one that was not pure. When the Revolution, fostered by the long injustice of men, burst like a fruit, what it rejected was the whole system of constraints which preserved being, and of force which protected man against himself—and such a system, though normal to the human being, had ruined itself by a surfeit of abuses. The Revolution, as we know, inaugurated the era of liberty. If, from the Edict of Milan down to the Declaration of the Rights of Man, human energy in the service of Christ lasted for fifteen centuries before going bankrupt, a century and a half—even less !—was sufficient for human liberty emancipated from Christ to plunge the world in a chaos of woes.

Souls nowadays would seem to be waiting for some

further deliverance, a genuine deliverance in the universalism of Christ or a sham deliverance in the universalism of Antichrist ; both may perhaps take place simultaneously in the divided world. The Catholic deliverance is a victory of love. Its greatest danger is from within : the spirit must not yield. It is being sorely tried ; it is being asked to provide from its own resources the order which the constraints of society formerly helped man to maintain within himself. Order is in the heart of sacred love. In God love proceeds from the Father and the uncreated Word. In us, who are made in the likeness of God, love must also proceed from truth ; otherwise it turns destructive ; it is expensive to deny the *Filioque*. In its *formalist* period (if I may hazard such an epithet), the modern world sinned in the first place against love, outraged the likeness of the Trinity in itself by attempting to impose a sterile form upon things, a word which did not *exhale* love. In its *liberal* period, it was by attempting in the first place to embrace all things in a love not emanating from truth that it outraged the likeness of God in itself, sinning then against the word, that is to say against the principle of love. And love suffers no less from that second sin.

There, however, is the danger which continues to threaten us. For we have witnessed several episodes of modernism and the struggle against it, but unforeseen episodes may still arise. Eastern thought, so far as it comes to the faith of Christ, will bring the Church abundant resources for the contemplative life ; but the danger which, even then, will attend such riches will still be a danger of mistrust with regard to the Word, to which the East, when it goes astray, unlike

99

the Extreme West, seems to prefer not practical action, but a formless speculation which is not infused contemplation and would fain be above reason. The abhorrence of Latinity is as worthless as the idolatry of it ; for many minds it is merely an ornamental façade concealing a fundamental intolerance of the *form of reason*.

Well ! the danger indicated may certainly be avoided, but on well-defined conditions. The East, like the West, needs the lessons of wisdom which orders all things in accordance with the hierarchies of nature and grace. I beg to be excused for reverting to a former essay [109]. " The fact is," I wrote, " that the order of reason, having ceased to be maintained under the order of charity, has become everywhere corrupted and is no longer fit for anything. The evil of rationalism has produced a discord between nature and the form of reason. It has now become exceedingly difficult to remain within the bounds of the human. You must place your stake either above reason and still for it, or below reason and against it. Now only the theological virtues and the supernatural gifts and infused contemplation are above reason. All the so-called supra-rational, which is not in charity, ultimately serves only animality. The hatred of reason will never be other than the revolt of the genus against the specific difference.

" The world, the world I mean for which Christ has not prayed, has made its choice beforehand. To set itself free from the *forma rationis*, to fly away from God, in an impossible metaphysical suicide, from the harsh and saving order appointed by the eternal Law, is the aspiration with which the flesh of the old Adam quivers, the aspiration of the Ancient of Ancients when he fell like lightning from the sky. . . .

" It is a mistake, however, to judge only according to nature. Grace is there with surprises in store. While this old world continues its downward career, the real new world is at hand, the secret invincible urge of divine sap in the mystic Body which endures and grows not old, the blessed awakening of souls at the prompting of the Virgin and the Spirit. O Wisdom striding in power from end to end of the world and making extremes meet! Installed in ancient errors and now affected by our follies, the East is as ailing as the distracted West and the bewildered Slav world. But on all sides we shall see, wherever the living faith takes root, the adhesion to what is truly above reason, to uncreated Truth and the wisdom of the Saints, simultaneously achieve—not without a strenuous effort certainly—the restoration of the very order of reason, implied as a condition by super-natural life. So the Gospel and philosophy, mysticism and metaphysics, the divine and the human go hand in hand. . . ."

30. When we think of Europe, more especially of the Mediterranean civilisation, we are dazzled by all the grandeur of its vocation and its past. One point, however, should hold our attention. Whatever the state of its intrinsic titles may be, the kind of historic monopoly which that civilisation enjoyed *in fact*, now seems to be severely shaken. It is important in this connection to understand thoroughly the significance of the war and the frightful rent it made. Benedict XV's remark about the suicide of Europe goes

further than one thinks. Europe has killed *its past*. Weep your eyes out over the gods of Hellas and the whole classical past, the immense secular body of profane Christian culture from which every European born into the world drew some sap of nourishing humanity and which supported him in life, educated and sustained him on all sides, now seems as it were inanimate. In fact those who received so much from it have now the sensation of receiving almost nothing at all. All the fragrance and beauty, the forms and values, the very pictures by which our ancestors lived, which made nature fraternal to them and the universe familiar, and which from generation to generation prepared us in them, have suddenly become remote and separate from us, entirely worthy of admiration and respect, but immovably fixed in what has ceased to be. This is undoubtedly the deepest cause of the great distress afflicting contemporary youth. It is strolling in its own humanity as in a museum : it sees its heart in the show-cases. Too many masterpieces. Is it surprising that it should want to smash the lot ? We are exotic to our very selves : is it surprising that nothing should strike us as exotic and that every human form indifferently should excite our curiosity— or merely bore us ?

Souls have been stripped bare. And the Church also in a sense is bare. All the wool and silk, all the riches of secular humanity with which the civilisation of a select part of the world once clothed and protected and sometimes burdened her, are falling in tatters. Such a garment is not the Church. It does not matter to her special life. But the magnificent lustre she sheds over the world should not blind us to the fact that the

Prince of this world is making the world more and more alien to her. Well ! She is not afraid of solitude ; if need be, she will inhabit the deserts and make them blossom. There she will find new raiment to adorn her.

I do not despair of Europe. The death I have referred to is not a real death. The deep springs of her life are still there, concealed but not dried up. But I do say that no purely human means—only the Church and the Faith can make them gush forth again. Europe will rise again only if she returns entirely to the feet of Christ. Then only will she be able to resume her function of serving the world by guiding it, not ruling it for her own advantage. Meanwhile the Church reminds us that, if our culture is Greco-Latin, our religion is not. The Church adopted such a culture, but did not subordinate herself to it. If the West, grown callous by an excess of pre-varications and abuse of grace, refuses for a time her influence, she will boldly turn to cultures developed under other skies—she alone can do so without too great a risk, because she has in her hands the means of making all things right in hearts of good-will. She is the mother and nurse of civilisation, and knows how to bring up a world.

And let it not be thought that she will ever abandon the superior virtues which she herself produced out of Hellenic and Latin culture. If she made such an extensive use of that culture, the very simple explana-tion still holds good ; like ancient Hebraism in the order of revelation, that culture had received from Providence in the order of reason a privilege which it would be shameful to deny ; it is the only culture in which human reason nearly succeeded. There was therefore nothing exceptional in its providing the supernatural life of the Church with choice human means. Again, for the perfect achievement of such success, the superior influences which only the Church herself could dispense were required. They alone enable reason truly to attain that universality in the natural order to which it tends by nature and which the infirmity of man ceaselessly denies it. It took centuries of Christian work and effort for the mind finally to emerge into the integral universalism which truth requires. St. Thomas Aquinas is the great exponent of such universalism developed in the intelligence under the light of faith and for that reason the Church has such a predilection for his doctrine and has made it, in the words of Benedict XV, *her own special doctrine*. It has been very justly observed and should be untiringly reiterated : " It is not Catholicism which is Thomist, it is Thomism which is Catholic and it is Catholic because it is universalist." [1] The metaphysics and theology of St. Thomas are expressed in a system of symbols and a Latin language—but the philosophy itself is no more bound to *Latinism* than to the physics of Aristotle or Ptolemy. It welcomes all being, because it is absolutely docile to being. Its structure being as hard as steel, it is as extensible as may be ; its discipline being the strictest possible, it enjoys the utmost freedom. By one of those paradoxes which Providence does not disdain and which are the effect of a superior logic, the least scholastic philosophy grew out of Scholasticism. It is now being invited to come forward and occupy the most advanced positions.

[1] H. Woroniecki.

Those who possess are, no doubt, indolent as a rule and allow their treasures to lie undisturbed ; Thomists are hard put to it not to diminish St. Thomas. And men, we know, lay hands on everything that descends from Heaven to appropriate it to their ephemeral interests and make it serve their private quarrels. But if the force of gravity and the contingencies of opinion attract every human system towards the divisions of earth, the faith and contemplation from which the doctrine of St. Thomas depends will always preserve it in universality as an intellectual instrument for the Church. That is the capital point : that philosophy is the universal Church's intellectual *instrument* and it is therefore as impossible for it ever to restrict the universality of truth as for Catholicism ever to restrict Catholicity.

It is the Church who preserves all the virtues of the West. She preserves them by making them universal, inasmuch as she makes use of them in her own peculiar intellectual and spiritual life and so extracts from their natural particularities an immortal substance which she incorporates in herself. I have said that the garment of profane culture which Europe had woven for her is becoming undone. It is not the garment which is now in question, but the body itself. All the eternal sap in the wisdom and riches of the West has been incorporated in the peculiar life of the Church. A whole rational organism with a universal value transcending place and time has so been constituted, which will endure for ever. St. Thomas is entrusted with the task of maintaining its unity.

Supernatural faith is in itself independent of all such treasures of reason. But if it is to spread and preserve itself among men, it must make use of them. To claim to strip it of them on the pretext of disencumbering it, would be the grossest absurdity. Because of the natural infirmity of reason, which lacks the divine guarantees of integrity and perfection peculiar to faith, it may well be that important virtualities of rational wisdom, philosophical or theological, have remained concealed or insufficiently developed in the speculation of the West ; we have much to receive under this head from our Slav brethren and a genuine Christian spirituality which, in spite of the schism, is still able to produce saints.[1] We have also something to receive from non-Christian forms of thought, nay, from all the errors of the world, which always hold some truth captive. Nevertheless, whatever shall be received will have to be assimilated into the truth, and the peculiar doctrine of the Church has behind it the authority of the Church herself unceasingly assisted by God not in her infallible definitions only, but also in the whole of her intellectual life. The influences of material causality, adaptations to any particular historic formation, affect absolutely nothing essential in such doctrine ; it is true and so transcends all variations in time and space. It developed in a particular region of the globe and in the course of so many centuries, but so far from suffering any historical or geographical *particularisation* on that account, is on the contrary, after a very long period of ripening, ready to furnish the means of a universal reconstruction.

31. Catholics are faced with a task of immense

[1] Cf. Appendix IX.

difficulty : we should not attempt to blink the fact. To ensure the triumph of the universalism of Christ, it is now necessary to make up for the deficiencies in the Christian education which many nations have failed to receive. By *adapting* Catholicism to their use ? If adaptation means change, we do not adapt truth, but adapt ourselves to it. By *adapting* them to Catholicism ? If adaptation means conformity to something alien, there is no need of adaptation to Catholicism, which is nowhere alien. Let me select a better word and say that a great work of *preparation* is required which will enable such nations to make the Gospel grow in the soil of their own peculiar civilisations.

Such a work is possible, because in spite of all the accidental differences (exaggerated out of all proportion, apparently, by many philologists and theorists), man and the human reason are everywhere alike. " What struck me most on my arrival in China," Père Lebbe told me, " was not the difference, but the resemblance." Moreover, there is no place in the world but contains some trace of God ; He has left His secret marks everywhere and they only need to be found.

Such a work is terribly difficult, because it must have a simultaneous regard, in matters which the human subject would only too willingly confuse, for the absolute unchanging truth and the relativity of every contingent kind of cultural development. One law reminds us that grace has a natural right over all natures and nations and that in all countries the house of God is the common natal house of everyone. Another law reminds us that every weakness in regard to error is paid for at a terrific price and that souls are not brought to the light by complaisance for darkness.

It demands a universal collaboration. God grant intellectual vocations among the converted of every race. And may they hasten before too many ruins and blood-stained corpses mark the earth ! It is their effort which will perfect the common task. But a Frenchman may be permitted to believe that his country has received a special call to such an undertaking, because France was born missionary. What other country has spent more blood, lavished more devotion on the missions ? The more one knows and admires other countries, the better one divines the importance of the message of France. A certain intellectual protectionism, which enjoins ignorance of one's neighbour on the pretext of conserving one's own strength, but is dictated in reality by a feeling of *bourgeois* thrift and standing on one's dignity, is a hindrance to the delivery of such a message. When it gets the better of it—without thereby being false to itself—its stark enthusiasm then excites everyone to the best of which he is capable. Has it ears to-day for the imperious complaints challenging on all sides its ancient generosity ? The world is asking France to spend its intellectual strength on the great enterprise for which God is waiting.

At a time when the illusory wisdom of the philosophers of this world is besieging every mind in all countries, is it conceivable that such an enterprise can possibly be accomplished without the help of the mind equipped to the uttermost ? It is not through the imprecise and the formless that it has any chance of succeeding, but by dint of precision, formal and formed energy. To set to work for it without the strongest doctrinal guarantees or to hope to find adequate weapons in the most primitive and least differentiated state of Christian thought or to seek to build upon philosophies alien to truth would be courting the risk of grave disappointment. We must insist upon it again and again ; it is the most highly developed, the most perfect form of Christian thought, the lofty wisdom under the aegis of the common Doctor of the Church, which must be mobilised in this campaign. It must be made to yield in appropriate forms of presentation, and by thorough sifting to meet the genuine requirements of every general problem, the intellectual values which every country in the world needs. It is the form which preserves whatever is universal and permanent, it alone can revive the West, give it back the free and living use of its spiritual riches, its tradition and culture ; it alone can also save the inheritance of the East and reconcile the two halves of the world. For it is not a case of irreducibly opposing one culture to another or of jumbling them all in one nameless confusion, but of using the finest and most active intellectual forms elaborated in the Church to assume and integrate in the light of the incarnate Word, without injuring in the least their natural individuation and autonomy, all the wise and good and truly human, and even divine, elements in the various historical civilisations and disciplines.

A crusade of the spirit, the spirit of crusaders ! Purely defensive positions, compromises, provisional withdrawals, partial truths are now of no avail. It is to a universal expansion of the mind that we are summoned through love. It is high time. The soul craves to adhere unreservedly to the absolutism of truth and charity. There will be men come forward free from every preoccupation but Christ. The Saints have foretold their coming.[1] They will make no exception of persons, nations or races. The ancient routine or modern prejudices, the peace of mind of the rich, the fate of literature and good taste, will concern them little. Distinguishing in all things light from darkness, they will undertake to reconcile human antagonisms in justice and to give man wholly back to God. Love will make them universal by grace as God is universal by nature and expand their minds to the measure of the divine intentions. If the world refuses to receive them, their work will nevertheless not be in vain : it will be fulfilled at all events in the invisible kingdom of the hearts of such as listen to them.

III. THE PRE-EMINENCE OF CONTEMPLATION

32. Action is subject to time in which it takes place and disappears and the law which governs action is rapidity. Our Lord preached for three years. But whether one be as inactive as the hermits or as active as the doctors and the apostles, action triumphs over time only so far as it descends from contemplation, which unites the spirit to eternity. Three years in the life of Our Lord inserted into the flux of our continuance the infinite efficiency of His blessed contemplation and so occupy the whole of time to the last day.

[1] St. Vincent Ferrer, the Blessed Grignon de Montfort.

The primacy of the spiritual would, as was indicated at the beginning of this chapter,[1] be but imperfectly appreciated, if we neglected to consider the part played by contemplation in human life and its superiority over the merely active life.

The Ancients knew that the contemplative life, in which man " burns to perceive the beauty of God " and " offers Him the sacrifice of his soul," is worth more than the active life. " Absolutely and of itself," says St. Thomas,[2] " the contemplative life is better than the active life." It tends more directly to divine charity, which is the essence of perfection.

By the active life, the Ancients understood two distinct things, which yet go together : exterior activity in the midst of men and the effort to attain perfection in the virtues. This moral effort, from which we are never exempt, is ordered to contemplation and union with God to which it disposes the individual[3] ; the exterior activity ought—according to the perfected order of human life—to proceed from contemplation and union with God.[4] To the extent that the order of charity still falls short of perfection in man, to that extent exterior activity, not proceeding as it ought from adhesion to God, runs the risk of squandering the substance of man in accordance with the rhythm of matter and impeding the progress by which, under the impulse of God, man builds himself ; but at the same time moral effort, combined with that activity, is a necessary means of such progress. So that the active life is useful or

[1] Cf. pp. 78-9.
[2] St. Thomas Aquinas, *Sum. Theol.*, ii–ii, 180, 1 ; 182, 2, ad 3 ; 182, 1.
[3] *Ibid.*, 180, 2.   [4] *Ibid.*, 182, 1, 3, 4 ; 188, 6.

harmful, may assist progress or compel retreat, according as one or other of these two aspects is predominant. Things then only go as they ought, if man, while steadily increasing the exercise of the virtues, simplifies his exterior activity, restricts it to what the order of charity requires, rids it of that sort of pertness and presumption that " vagabond, disorderly and childish manner " [110] which is an illusion of life.

Again, once he has submitted to the habitual discipline of the gifts of the Holy Ghost and to the extent that he participates in the perfect life, then and to that extent the exterior activity proceeds in him, as it ought, from adhesion to God, supervenes by way of addition, not subtraction,[1] then, so far from being a deficiency or an impediment, it is a superabundance. So the whole multitude of everyday actions, required by the necessities of human life and intercourse among men, became in the hands of the Blessed Virgin a dust of stars gathered in the sky. The movement of the active life is then reversed ; whereas it helped to make the ascent to God, it now descends from God. Then, and then only, according to its particular vocation and the mission it has received, can the creature perform the prodigies of activity which astound us in certain Saints, triumphs of grace in which man is a mere tool in the hands of Omnipotence and of which the most colossal achievements of our natural energy are but a fleeting counterfeit.

Such is the immutable order which no agitation can impair—an order which demands a whole succession of renunciations and deaths, because it is the consequence of our destination to a supernatural end.

---

[1] St. Thomas Aquinas, *Sum. Theol.*, ii–ii, 182, 1, ad 3.

Only a few so much as begin to follow it. And how many proceed to the end? Ultimately, no doubt, everything is returned to them in a way—transfigured in the liberty of the children of God, *qui spiritu Dei aguntur*. They bear witness, however, that even infused contemplation does not raise them to participation in the life of Christ and the three divine Persons, except in a night hard as death in which Love deprives them of all their human ways of acting. And truly, before ascending to such a height through some eminent grace, they must have acted by themselves, by themselves made use of all their faculties forcibly directed towards God—it is indeed the fundamental error of quietism that it professes to obtain by merely human effort a passivity which God alone can give. Nevertheless the very force of their will must have applied itself rather to appeasing their natural activity, to making it fast, than to overexciting it in a kind of athletic development. For that summons to perfection, which love makes to everyone but which only they have heard, directed them from the very beginning to a divine union transcending all the energies of nature.

They are scattered and unknown these friends of God, but it is they who redeem souls and are the mainstay of the world, by making good in their own persons whatever deficiency there was in the Passion of their Master. But do they preserve human history from jeopardy? If the world, in spite of everything, has for some centuries past achieved an organic progress and enabled men to raise themselves in accordance with the spirit, it is because in the structure of its functions and states, in its scale of values and the form of its culture, it continued to be dominated, whatever the morals of the great majority may have been, by the essential order of human life, the order directed to perfection, which the Saints alone fully realise.

The modern world has completely reversed that essential order of human life. Exterior activity began three centuries ago and more to absorb the whole life of man, because in reality the world then turned to the conquest and practical utilisation of matter away from union with God through faith and love. Conversion to perishable goods, the definition of mortal sin, gradually became the general attitude of civilisation.

The Church, however, has always maintained in her teaching and practice the primacy of theological activity and contemplation. She remembers Moses praying for the armies of Joshua with Aaron and Hur supporting his arms, which could not droop without endangering the victory [111]. "What use," asked St. John of the Cross whom she has just proclaimed a doctor, "are those who prefer activity and think that they can conquer the world by their preaching and exterior works? What do they do? A little more than nothing, sometimes absolutely nothing, sometimes even harm [112]." For the "mixed life," which St. Thomas declares to be superior to the merely contemplative life, is not the life in which action diverts from contemplation, but the life in which contemplation itself superabounds in action.

Contemplation alone discovers the value of charity. Without it, it is only known by hearsay. With it, it is known by experience. By love and in love, it proclaims that God is love. Then man lets God do in him as He will, allows himself to be bound, because he is in love. He is free because he loves. Whatever lacks the taste of love loses all its savour for him.

Because of this love in which it consumes our life, contemplation alone realises in us universality, makes the soul Catholic in spirit and in truth. As it transcends all the intellectual and moral virtues, prudence, understanding and art, so it also transcends all particularisms, attunes the soul to the unity of the mystic Body of Christ, disharmonises it with every more contracted unity. Through it Christ, dwelling in them that love Him, gives their hearts a sort of Eucharistic amplitude.

Without contemplation, every philosophical and theological doctrine, even true, becomes sectarian ; all forms of even honourable zeal mere rivalries. Because it makes man one single spirit with God, it really makes unity in man and among men. It proceeds from the gift of wisdom and the beatitude of the peacemakers is the privilege of such a gift.

33. The works which penetrate furthest into the future are those which the Spirit of God ordains in silence and leads as His freedom wills. The operation of grace is preparing great things in a youth stirred by a yearning for the absolute, the more ardent of whom are turning to-day to God. A stern contest is being waged on the frontiers of the mind and art and philosophy. Such an activity is naturally peculiar to a small group : so far from seeking the collaboration of all, it demands rather a measure of solitude. All that can be wished for in that sphere in the way of broad union is a union in charity, which would spare those who are bearing the brunt of the enemy's attack

many an additional blow from their brethren in the faith.

In other spheres, however, another kind of broad union is practicable, union in the work itself, and this invites every kind of assistance. I wrote some years ago with reference to Catholics who were resolved to live their faith regardless of modern errors and to serve the interests of Christ before all other interests : " However acute their oppositions may and ought to be on matters which from the human point of view are sometimes very important, they will always have for common principles not only the dogmas of the faith, but also the intellectual directions, *all* the intellectual directions, both speculative and practical, maternally given by Rome and received in a spirit of lively and filial docility. It looks as though the time had come for them to make a truly Catholic, that is to say universal, synthesis, to construct, to gather together, to insist everywhere on the positive, and with that object first to reconcile in their minds, under the indispensable light of theological wisdom (otherwise there is nothing to hope for), aspects which, although too long kept apart, are in reality complementary, doctrinal absolutism and evangelical daring, fidelity to pure truth and compassion for sick souls, tradition where needed, revolution where needed. . . . *Miseri-cordia et veritas obviaverunt sibi . . .*" [113].

With such a programme of unqualified adhesion to every pontifical direction, Catholics, if they so desired and whatever their differences in other spheres, could usefully unite in accordance with the constantly reiterated desire of the Sovereign Pontiffs and work in harmony. Such a union is possible, in the first place, in the order of knowledge. The desire to become better acquainted with the doctrine of the Church, of which so many baptised persons are so lamentably ignorant, is apparent on all sides and to be fortified against hydra-headed error by a serious philosophical and theological training. For the past fifty years the Popes have been imploring Catholics all to have recourse to St. Thomas Aquinas. Have such urgent entreaties been met with a sufficiently generous love of truth? If in the interval a unanimous effort had been made to reform the mind under the inspiration of the common Doctor, Catholics would be commanding every highway in the world. Fierce assaults are preparing against the Church at the moment, while many minds are threatened by a sort of syncretism, indulgent to every kind of error. Recourse to arms brooks no delay.

The union mentioned is equally practicable in the sphere of action, on condition that the proximate ends of the action contemplated are sufficiently universal. Whether it be a question of co-operating in such a spiritual restoration of Christendom—and this would seem to be the great task of to-day—or assisting in the work of evangelisation, in the immense labour of the missions at home and abroad; or rediscovering the principles of Christian politics and combating laicism and its laws; or preparing for the establishment of a Christian social order and opposing social conditions contrary to the justice and the spirit of the Gospel; or practising works of spiritual and corporal mercy, or bringing succour to all the suffering members of Christ, not only to the poor and sick, but also to so many ardent hearts exasperated in error by false doctrines, the iniquity of this God-less world, the aridity and egoism of orthodox religious people—there is no lack of work calling for the co-operation of Catholics because they are Catholics. It would be sufficient if all who have been working for years in separate teams in a multitude of admirably various and necessarily independent tasks got to know one another. The new forms which might arise would take their place in that concert, whose supreme rule would be the integral teaching imparted by the Papacy. A harmonised activity, so proceeding from the spirit of faith, the love of Christ in His Church and a great devotion to His word unceasingly transmitted by his Vicar, would, so far from diverting souls from the life of union with God, impel them rather the other way. That is indeed the sort of common action which the life of union with God itself demands. *Negotium justum suscipit necessitas charitatis.*[1] Making its way little by little, it would soon be followed by immense results for the extension of the kingdom of God. The work makes poor progress merely because of the lack of union among the workers.

34. Still more necessary, however, than such a union of all in action—and constituting also a superior condition of it—is the invisible union of a few in contemplation, in that wisdom which can do all things : " and remaining in herself the same, reneweth all things, and through nations conveyeth herself into holy souls, she maketh the friends of God and prophets."[2]

[1] " The love of truth seeks a holy repose, the necessity of love accepts a just task," *otium sanctum quaerit charitas veritatis, negotium justum suscipit necessitas charitatis*. (St. Augustine, *De Civit. Dei*, xix, 19.)
[2] Wisdom vii, 27.

This is what the anguish of the present clamours for in the first place. The world is crying out for saints. If Catholics do not give it what it wants, so much the worse for them and for everybody ; it will be revenged upon them and go for consolation to the devil. The successive crises among them during the last twenty-five years reveal a painful inheritance of weakness. The condemnations they have entailed must be considered as the liquidation of the nineteenth century. God clearly wants something new.

But, in the first place and above all, He asks us to restore within ourselves the essential order which the modern world has shattered. " St. Paul, who came in signs and wisdom, says that he came neither in signs nor wisdom," [1] only in the virtue of the folly of the cross. That Jew, destitute of everything, whom God consumed with love, carries Europe and all the Christian centuries in his arms. And what does he say ? . . . " I bow my knees to the Father of Our Lord Jesus Christ, of Whom all paternity in heaven and earth is named, that he would grant you, according to the riches of his glory, to be strengthened by his Spirit with might unto the inward man. That Christ may dwell by faith in your hearts : that being rooted and founded in charity, you may be able to comprehend, with all the saints, what is the breadth, and length, and height, and depth. To know also the charity of Christ, which surpasseth all knowledge, that you may be filled unto all the fulness of God." [2] However few they may be, those who take to heart the lesson of St. Paul and strive to live only to be one day filled with that fulness, fulfil the design for which

[1] Pascal.   [2] Ephesians iii. 14-19.

we were born. For " after all, we have been created only for that love. In the evening of this life, it is on love we shall be judged " [114].

35. Now what purpose does this book serve ? Contemplative minds already knew, better than its author, everything it attempts to explain. Others will be none the wiser.

Anyone who does not understand to-day, may perhaps understand to-morrow. And again, as Pascal says, we have not been given the task of securing the triumph of truth, but of fighting on its behalf.

APPENDICES

I. ON THE THEORY OF THE "DIRECT" POWER IN TEMPORALIBUS

"A FEW theologians, in the course of history, have even pushed the enthusiastic conviction of the rights of the Church to the extent of claiming for her directly all power on earth. The *ne scandalizemus eos* by which Our Lord motives His pure and gracious concession in paying the didrachma appeared to them the only possible limit to the rights of the Mother of the redeemed. . . ." (Père Humbert Clérissac, *Le Mystère de l'Église*). The teaching of Leo XIII in the encyclicals *Sapientiae Christianae* and *Immortale Dei* would seem to convict them definitely of error and in any event absolutely rejects the gross exaggerations into which certain fourteenth and fifteenth century canonists had fallen : proceeding to the opposite extreme to the regalian pretensions of the lawyers, they insisted that every right, every lawful dominion and legitimate possession were enclosed as in a box in the breast of the Sovereign Pontiff, in such a way as to enable the latter to intervene directly and of course in questions of property within the jurisdiction of the civil law and that an appeal lay to him as of course from every sentence pronounced by the secular judges ; they held the power of pagan princes over infidel peoples to be unlawful and denied in short the lawfulness of terrestrial powers based on natural law. Yet the Church no more constitutes such lawfulness than grace constitutes nature. (Cf. A. Baudrillart, "Des idées qu'on se faisait au quatorzième siècle sur le droit d'intervention du Souverain Pontife en matière politique,'' in *Revue d'histoire et de littérature religieuse*, vol. iii, 1898 ; Jean Rivière, *Le problème de l'Église et de l'État au temps de Philippe le Bel*, 1926 ; E. Dublanchy, '' Turrecremata et le pouvoir du Pape dans les questions temporelles,'' *Revue Thomiste*, January—March 1923 ; Turrecremata, *Summa Ecclesiae* ; Bellarmine, *De Summo Pontifice*, lib. v.)

Not all the partisans of the theory of the direct power over the temporal fell into such exaggerations, but they were concerned to attribute to the Church a high dominion over the universality of temporal sovereignties *in respect even of the temporal good to be procured*, to the end that kings should be considered solely and simply as ministers or delegates of the Church *in temporalibus* and depend directly on her authority in that particular sphere. Must not the temporal sovereignty of Christ have been transmitted by Him to the Church and Peter no less than His spiritual sovereignty ?

And it is perfectly true, as has already been observed, that the kingship of Christ is not only spiritual but also temporal. Raised by the hypostatic union above all human beings, possessing a consummate and complete infused knowledge which makes His mind perfect in the highest degree and allows Him to rule the world universally (cf. C. V. Héris, *Rev. des sc. phil. et théol.*, July 1926), Christ, as Man, has received from God an absolute right over all created things to govern them in accordance with His universal ends. '' It would be a disgraceful error,'' Pope Pius XI wrote recently in the encyclical *Quas Primas* (11th December, 1925), to deny the authority of the Christ-Man over any civil matter whatsoever, inasmuch as He has received from the Father so absolute a right over created things that everything is subject to His will.''

'' Nevertheless,'' the encyclical continues, '' throughout the whole of His earthly life, He absolutely refrained from exercising any authority of the kind, and scorning the possession and administration of human things, abandoned them then, as He abandons them to-day, to their owners. This is admirably expressed in the verses : *Non eripit mortalia, qui regna dat caelestia*" [from the hymn *Crudelis Herodes*, in the Office of the Epiphany].

We are thereby given a hint of a great mystery of the historic life of His mystical Body and the perpetual urgency of the phrase : " My kingdom is not of this world," the profound explanation of which is precisely the redeeming mission of Our Lord. Whatever the conventional value of their arguments may have been, and even supposing that their now long forgotten opinions, reduced to their most formal elements, could possibly be reconciled with the truth on which Leo XIII was later to shed such a flood of light, the partisans of the direct power over the temporal should never have omitted the correction which at any rate suggests itself immediately and which the encyclical of Christ the King so justly indicates. One may have a right and not exercise it, a sword and keep it sheathed. *Mitte gladium tuum in vaginam. . . .* Would it be proper for the Church to make effective use, even in the most tactful way and with the highest motives, of a power which her Master refused to exercise ? She never has in fact used such a power. Every intervention of hers in the temporal, even when she assumed the inheritance of the declining Empire in order to make Europe, has invariably proceeded from the indirect power only (not to mention cases involving only a human and alienable right, such as might have been assumed by bishops, in the absence of the political authority, to defend the life of States against invasions or that conferred by an arbitration spontaneously invited by opposing parties).[1]

[1] Leaving out of account also cases in which the Pope himself proceeded to act (diplomatically or in the field) as temporal sovereign of the Papal States.

The reason is that for the Church, as for the Lord Jesus, the redemptive mission predominates over every other consideration. The Church is bound to make good whatever defect there was in His Passion. He came to suffer and redeem, not to dominate, and it will continue to be so in future ages until His kingdom comes.

The Popes from the eleventh to the fourteenth century testified by their teaching and action, as heads of the Church, not to the theory of the direct power but to the doctrine of the indirect power and the supremacy of the spiritual over the temporal, itself sovereign and independent in its own domain.[1] It may, however, well be wondered if the Middle Ages, in affirming so magnificently the right, were not too optimistic in regard to the fact and seeking with still excessive confidence in man and the world the realisation on earth of the primacy of the spiritual. Be that as it may, it must not be forgotten that the doctrine of the direct power over the temporal is a mere theological opinion rejected by all modern theologians. It has been alluded to here simply for the sake of completeness and there will be no further mention of it in this essay.

Certain declarations (by Mgr. Ireland or Cardinal Gibbons) have recently been recalled denying the Pope the right " to impose his will in purely civil matters." They should be regarded, let it be observed in conclusion, as a refusal to concede to the Pope a direct power over civil matters (if, for example, the Pope were to intervene in the electoral system of the United States on the ground of the political good of the citizens, a thing which he would never be tempted to do) and, clearly, not in any way as a repudiation of his indirect power over the temporal on the ground of the divine interests of which he is the custodian.

[1] Cf. G. de Lagarde, *Recherches sur l'esprit politique de la Réforme.*

II. POLITICS AND THEOLOGY

" Were we to say that politics (political science and political prudence) is a kind of physics and a kind of art of the social good, a separate branch of ethics, a science and actual practice of the conditions of prosperity of the State determined by observation from the sole point of view of ' natural laws,' and susceptible of having moral considerations subsequently and supererogatorily engrafted upon them, we should be guilty of a capital error. The end of the terrestrial State is the *totum bene vivere* of mankind on this earth ; a temporal good, no doubt, but one which is not only of the *material* order, but also and pre-eminently of the *moral and spiritual order.* The science and practice of the good conduct of the State are therefore inseparable from the exact knowledge of the ends of human life.

" This is the very reason why St. Thomas, basing himself upon Aristotle but surpassing him infinitely, could assure in doctrine the total subordination of politics to ethics before referred to, and alone—applying with perfect exactitude the very true principle : ' The good of the whole is more divine than the good of the part,' [1] which the pagans constantly tended to convert into an idolatry of the State—show on the one hand that everything relating to man, *considered formally as part of the State,* can be referred to the good of the State, but on the other hand that there is an aspect in man in accordance with which man, being referred directly to God, escapes such a political ordination and himself possesses the dignity of a whole more eminently than the entire physical world, inasmuch as God is much more intimately the end of a soul than of the whole universe of bodies. For this reason, also, according to St. Thomas, a private individual can be a

[1] Because the whole as such *is* more than the part and so is nearer to the first Being.

good citizen (*civis communis*, if not *civis praeclarus*), without being morally good *simpliciter* (it is enough if he possess the civic virtues and be ordered to the common good), whereas the Prince performs his political function well, his princely function, only on condition of being a virtuous man purely and simply, not only in the political order, but also in the whole order of the moral life. For he must be the incarnation of the common good. . . .

" Integral political science, however great the part observation and induction may properly play in it, is not only superior in kind to inductive science, to a merely physical observation of facts and empirical sequences (so-called sociology, as Durkheim interprets it), but also superior in kind to philosophy ; to be truly complete it must have a reference to the domain of theology, and it is precisely as a theologian that St. Thomas wrote his *De regimine principum* ; ends, indeed, being in the practical order what principles are in the speculative order, the knowledge of human actions and of the good conduct of the human State in particular can exist as an integral science, as a complete body of doctrine, only if related to the ultimate end of the human being. An Aristotle, no doubt, in spite of the deficiency indicated, could trace the outline of a political *philosophy*, part of a moral *philosophy* itself suspended to the doctrine of the supreme Good (of a natural supreme good, such as it might be conceived by a pagan, and still very obscurely). Every political *philosophy* is therefore, like every moral *philosophy*, a sort of abstract limit, the science of the *natural* laws governing human action. Man, however, is not in fact in a purely *natural* state, but in the state of nature fallen and redeemed ; the rule of conduct governing individual and social life cannot therefore leave the supernatural order out of account." (*Une opinion sur Charles Maurras et le devoir des Catholiques*, pp. 40–45.)

III. THE DOCTRINE OF THE INDIRECT
   POWER AND THE DOCTRINE OF THE TWO
   SWORDS

The doctrine of the two swords, as conceived by a
St. Bernard and a St. Thomas Aquinas, meant that the
Church has the temporal sword only in the sense in which
one is said to *have* that which one can direct the use of.
To be able to give orders to a power is in a way to possess
such a power. When St. Bernard wrote with reference to
the temporal sword : " It, too, is yours and it may be
drawn at a sign from you, although not by your hand.
. . . Both swords belong to the Church, the spiritual as
well as the material : the material sword is to be drawn in
defence of the Church, the spiritual by the Church, the
spiritual by the hand of the priest, the material by the
soldier, but at a sign from the priest and on the order of
the Emperor " (*De Consideratione*, iv, 3, 7), and when St.
Thomas and the most distinguished theologians of his
time, basing themselves upon that famous text, taught that
the Church possesses *the two swords* (" The spiritual for
execution only, but the temporal also to the extent that
it can order it to be drawn "—St. Thomas in iv *Sentent.*,
Dist. 37, expositio textus), they intended simply to affirm
that the spiritual sword can and ought to direct the
temporal sword (natural law is sufficient to justify the
lawfulness of drawing it) because of spiritual interests
themselves and with a view to the supernatural end,
and so merely professed the theory of the indirect power.
(There is, however, a difference to be observed between
the old and the modern philosophers of *the point of view*
in the manner of considering and presenting this theory.
The former, taking a more metaphysical point of view and
considering in the first place the subordination of ends, laid
the greater stress on the general subjection of the temporal

to the spiritual and of kings to the Supreme Pontiffs in view of the ultimate supernatural end to be attained. The latter, taking a more juridical point of view and considering in the first place what delimitations to draw in practice, discuss the indirect power in a narrower sense, restricted to express interventions by the Church in temporal matters *ratione peccati*, and lay the greater stress on the liberty which the Church, such special cases apart, leaves to temporal powers.)

The doctrine of the two swords is susceptible of another interpretation and may assert for the Church not only the right to check temporal sovereigns *ratione peccati*—not to mention the right to appoint them in case of necessity and to relieve the pressing needs of peoples who run the risk of deviating spiritually if they are not governed— but also an exalted supremacy over the temporal *as such* which would make sovereigns, illegitimate without her consent, mere delegates. This is again the doctrine of the direct power over the temporal (cf. Appendix I, *ante*). These two different interpretations of the " possession of the two swords " are often confused in the theories of canonists towards the end of the Middle Ages and the confusion does not make the discussion any easier.

Before Bellarmine, Cardinal Giovanni di Turrecremata (*Summa Ecclesiae*) and Cajetan (Tommaso de Vio) had already explained as precisely as could be desired the theological doctrine of the indirect power. Cajetan, for example, in his *Apologia de authoritate Papae*, Tract ii, c. 13, ad 8, writes as follows : " The power of the Pope with regard to spiritual things is direct in relation to the supreme end *simpliciter* of the human race ; there are therefore two characteristics of his power, one of not being direct with regard to temporal things, the other of being, with regard to temporal things, in relation to spiritual things. This is because everything, including temporal things, ought, without a doubt, to be ordered to the ultimate end by him whose function it is to direct all men to one end and such is the Vicar of Christ." In his Commentary on the *Summa Theologica* with reference to the following passage from St. Thomas Aquinas (*Sum. Theol.*, ii–ii, 60, 6, ad 3) : "*The secular power is subject to the spiritual power as the body is to the soul ; for this reason there is no usurpation of power, if the spiritual superior intervenes in the temporal order with regard to things in which the secular power is subject to it or which are ceded to the spiritual by the secular power,*" he writes : " The soul governs the body in a triple order of causality : by efficient causality, for it is the cause of the corporal movements of the animal, by formal causality, for it is the form of the body, by final causality, for the body exists for the soul. It is the same, proportionately, with the spiritual power in relation to the secular power : the power which disposes of spiritual things has a formal part to play in relation to the power which disposes of secular things ; the latter are ordered to spiritual and eternal things as to their end : and the highest end corresponding to the most exalted agent, it is for the spiritual power to move and direct the temporal power and all that pertains to it to the supreme spiritual end.

" The consequence is that the spiritual power by its very nature has authority over the temporal power *in view of the spiritual end ;* such are the things in which the temporal power is subject to the spiritual, and this is what St. Thomas means when he writes ' *with respect to things in which the secular power is subject to the spiritual power.*' That means that the secular power is not subject absolutely and in every respect to the spiritual power : for instance, in the civil order the Governor of the State must be obeyed, in the military order the Commander of an army, rather than the Bishop, who has no business to meddle in such matters unless in relation to spiritual things (*nisi in ordine ad spiritualia*). But should anything whatsoever in temporal things in any way jeopardise eternal salvation, the prelate then intervening in that domain by a command or a prohibition is not thrusting his scythe into another man's harvest but legitimately exercising his own authority : because all secular powers are subject on that score to the spiritual power. Such is the meaning to be given to the first paragraph of St. Thomas's answer in which he shows in what way the spiritual power is judge of temporal things. The second paragraph : *with respect to things which are ceded to the spiritual by the temporal power*, refers to prelates who, by the gift of kings, in many places possess both jurisdictions."

Bellarmine (*De potestate Summi Pontificis*, cap. v), after defining the classic doctrine of the indirect power, " By the words *direct* and *indirect* . . . we understand . . . that the pontifical power is by nature and specifically spiritual and therefore directly concerned with spiritual matters as its primary object : but indirectly, that is in relation to spiritual things, reductively, and by necessary consequence so to speak, it is concerned with temporal things, as its secondary object, to which this spiritual power is not converted unless in special cases, as Innocent III says," refers explicitly to Turrecremata, Cajetan, Vittoria, Dominic Soto and several others. He attributes the expression " indirect power " to Innocent IV, that Pope having employed the adverb *indirect* to indicate the way in which the spiritual power affects temporal things. The word, as M. Jean Rivière points out (*op. cit.* pp. 39 and 54), was, however, already in current use in the time of Innocent IV and familiar to the commentators of the early thirteenth century. Vincent the Spaniard, for example, who wrote about 1216, commenting upon the words of Innocent III, " For we do not intend to judge the fee," adds " *Directe* ; sed *indirecte* cognoscendo an peccet et inducendo ad poenitentiam . . . et ita per consequentiam feudum restituet." The distinction was taken up again by Innocent IV, who unequivocally asserted the indirect power over the temporal *ratione peccati*. Historians may discuss the personal inclinations of St. Gregory VII, Innocent IV and Boniface VIII to the end of time. Whatever their private views may have been, the only doctrine they professed as Popes was the doctrine of the indirect power.

Bellarmine's doctrine was taken up again by Suarez. The following statement by the latter should be remembered (Vivès ed., vol. v, p. 366, No. 3) : " There are not two powers in the Supreme Pontiff, but *one only* relating directly to spiritual things and by way of consequence to temporal things."

IV. THE THREE MEANINGS OF THE WORD "DEMOCRACY."

" Philosophy must distinguish three meanings in the word democracy or everything will be hopelessly confused :

" (a) Democracy as a social tendency,[1] recommended by the Popes (*demophily*, Christian democracy),[2] simply the ardent desire to procure for the working classes, more than ever oppressed in the modern world, the human

---

[1] What Leo XIII also calls *Christian democracy*. I had written *social democracy* to indicate that it was a question of the *social* relations of men among themselves and not of the form of *political* government. My attention was drawn to the fact that the words might lead to misunderstanding, Leo XIII having found fault with them, although in quite a different sense, so far as they signified the socialist or communist system (encyclical *Graves de Communi*). The expression had therefore better be discarded : " democracy as a social tendency " is, I hope, absolutely unequivocal.

[2] " Although democracy, from the very meaning of the word and the usage of philosophers, indicates popular government, nevertheless, in the present context, it is so employed that it has lost all political connotation and simply means *this very beneficial Christian action in regard to the people*." Leo XIII, encyclical *Graves de Communi*.

conditions of life required not only by charity, but also and in the first place by justice. (Continuing in such a direction, we shall doubtless arrive at a radical criticism of our economic régime, such as has already been partially effected by several Catholic writers.)

" It is regrettable that the zeal displayed by the Catholic masses in the defence of the social order and the struggle against revolutionary elements have coincided only too often with an omission to observe this elementary duty and a terrifying lack of attention to the injunctions of Leo XIII.

" (b) *Political democracy* (πολιτεία), as conceived by Aristotle and St. Thomas, exemplified, for instance, in the old Swiss democracy and considered by the Church and philosophy as a legally possible form of government (indicated or counter-indicated in fact, according to historic conditions and circumstances).

" (c) *Democratism*, or democracy as conceived by Rousseau, that is to say the religious myth of Democracy, an entirely different thing from the legitimate democratic régime (πολιτεία). (This myth also necessitates in the *Social Contract* a theory of the three classic systems, monarchical, aristocratic and democratic, which is equally false and pernicious.) Democracy in this sense becomes confused with the dogma of the Sovereign People,[1] which, combined with the dogma of the general Will and Law as the expression of Number, constitutes, in the extreme, the error of political pantheism (the multitude—God).

" It must, however, be observed that what makes the condition of nations in modern times so tragic is that in fact, in concrete reality, the religious myth of Democracy has everywhere invaded and contaminated political democracy and even every actual form of government. The effort of the mind should be directed to making the

[1] That is to say of the people as perpetual possessor and *sole lawful possessor* of sovereignty.

necessary discriminations and, while taking account of the relations of fact found in history, should devote itself to the task of securing the re-establishment of conditions essential to a practical renovation which will be successful only if it is complete." (*Une opinion sur Charles Maurras et le devoir des Catholiques*, pp. 25–29.)

I would add that in the vocabulary of St. Thomas, democracy as legitimate form of government ((*b*) above) is not called democracy, but Republic (*politia*). It is a sort of *mixed system*, in which the democratic principle which, in the abstract, would tend to the supremacy of mere numbers, (" Democracy, that is to say the supremacy of the populace, when *the mass of the people* through weight of numbers oppresses the rich," *De Regim. princ.*, i, 1) is tempered by the aristocratic principle (the supremacy of the pre-eminent in value or virtue) and above all by the oligarchic principle (the supremacy of the pre-eminent in riches or power). (Cf. *Comment in Polit. Aristotelis*, iv, vii.) It is therefore more exactly an *ameliorated democracy*. (Cf. Marcel Demongeot, *Le meilleur régime politique selon St. Thomas*, Paris, Blot, 1928, and the very valuable articles by D. Lallement : " La doctrine politique de St. Thomas d'Aquin," *Revue de Philosophie*, July–August, 1927, September–October, 1927, January–February, 1929.)

As for the word *democracy*, it signifies in St. Thomas both the corrupt form of the *politia* and the abstract democratic principle.

V. ON LIBERALISM

Liberalism, as is commonly known, is a condemned error.[1] It was liberalism above all which Pius IX had in

[1] Cf. the encyclicals *Mirari vos* (Gregory XVI) ; *Quanta cura* (Pius IX) ; *Immortale Dei, Sapientiae Christianae, Libertas, praestantissimum* (Leo XIII) ; *Pascendi* (Pius X) and *Ubi Arcano Dei* (Pius XI). The words " *liberal* " and " *liberalism* " are to be understood here, not as

mind when he condemned the following proposition :
" The Roman Pontiff can and ought to reconcile himself
to, and compromise with, progress, liberalism and modern
civilisation " (*Syllabus*, prop. 80). Leo XIII summed up
the whole error in a single phrase, " Every man is a law
unto himself,"[1] which is merely the fundamental axiom
of Rousseau in the social order and Kant in the moral
order : " Obey nobody but yourself " ; it expresses the
essential claim of modern immanentism.

Pope Leo has developed a full and important doctrine
on this question, more particularly in the Encyclicals
Immortale Dei and *Libertas, praestantissimum*, the importance
of which is as urgent as ever.

Liberty, he declares, recalling the teaching of St. Thomas,

they may be used to describe any particular political party, but in the
strict sense given to them in the language of theologians. The distinction
was very precisely expressed by Leo XIII, who also added the wish that
some other name might be found to describe political parties (Letter
of Cardinal Rampolla to the Archbishop of Bogota, 6th April, 1900 :
" Wherefore, in the present case, there should be borne in mind what
the Supreme Congregation of the Holy Office enjoined on the bishops
of Canada on the 29th August, 1877, namely that the Church, in
condemning liberalism, had no intention of condemning each and all
of the political parties described as liberal.

" I have also said as much myself in a letter addressed to the bishop
of Salamanca, at the instance of the Supreme Pontiff, on the 17th
February, 1891, adding, however, the following conditions : Catholics
who describe themselves as liberals must in the first place sincerely
adhere to every essential point of doctrine taught by the Church and
be disposed to admit whatever the Church may teach in the future :
moreover they will not set before themselves anything that the Church
has explicitly or implicitly condemned ; finally, as often as circumstances
may require, they will not refuse, and it is indeed their duty, openly
to proclaim that their objects are in full conformity with the doctrines
of the Church. It was also said in the same letter that it was desirable
that Catholics chose and adopted some other form of description to
indicate the political parties to which they belonged for fear that the
name of liberals assumed by them might mislead or astonish the faithful : but that it was not permissible to brand with a theological censure,
still less to denounce as heretical, liberalism understood in a different
sense from that defined by the Church in condemning it and that so
long as the Church should have given no other indications ").

[1] Encyclical *Libertas, praestantissimum*.

is the privilege of creatures endowed with mind or reason [1] ;
it is essentially the faculty of being able to choose between
the means conducing to the end, for he who has the
faculty of choosing one thing among many is master of his
actions. The possibility of choosing *evil* is not of the
essence of liberty, it is a defect peculiar to *our* liberty :
" The faculty of committing sin is not a liberty, but a
servitude " : and so *whosoever committeth sin is the servant
of sin*,[2] because he suffers an alien impulse, contrary to the
internal principle of action which is the peculiar characteristic of the human being, that is to say reason.[3]

Because of its imperfection—and because, being subject
to becoming, we must in all things begin with the imperfect
and little by little grow up to adult age—human liberty
needs to be protected : that is the important thing. " Such
being the condition of human liberty, it needed protection ; it needed help and assistance capable of directing
all its movements towards the good and diverting them
from evil : otherwise free will would have been a very
harmful thing to man." And in the first place it needed a
law, or *ordinance of reason*, a rule of what to do or what not to
do. " Nothing more absurd or perverse could be said or
imagined than the statement that man, being naturally
free, ought to be exempt from all law ; if it were so, the
consequence would be that it is necessary for liberty not to
be in accordance with reason : whereas it is the contrary
which is true, namely that man ought to be subject to law

[1] St. Thomas, *Sum. Theol.*, i, 59, 3 . . . *wherever you have mind
(intellectus), there you have free will* ; i, 83, 1 . . . *that a man should
have free will is a necessary consequence from the very fact of his being a rational
creature* ; i–ii, 17, 1, ad 2 . . . *the root of liberty as subject is the will,
but as cause it is the reason.*

[2] St. John viii. 34. Leo XIII is here quoting the commentary of
St. Thomas.

[3] The possibility of falling into error is to reason as the possibility
of choosing evil is to free will. *Liberty to make a mistake* is a defect of
the rational nature, not a privilege of the mind as such or of the liberty
of the spirit.

precisely because he is by nature free. . . . Of its very nature then and considered from any angle whatever, in individuals or societies, in superiors no less than in subordinates, human liberty implies the necessity of obedience to a supreme eternal rule, which is no other than the authority of God in His commandments or prohibitions to us. This perfectly proper sovereignty, so far from destroying or impairing liberty in any degree, on the contrary protects it and brings it to its perfection. For the true perfection of every being consists in pursuing and attaining its end : now the supreme end to which human liberty should aspire is God." [1]

If, therefore, we are to attain in the end a perfect liberty (which is to be realised in its fulness only in Heaven and of which only the Saints, *qui spiritu Dei aguntur*, have a shadowy indication here below), our very nature—our nature perfected by grace, inasmuch as it has pleased God ·to raise it to the supernatural order—solicits, in order to attain that end, the regulative control of the divine law, both natural and revealed, and the educative constraints of the human State and the Church of Christ. In the words of Cajetan before referred to,[2] to attain his supernatural happiness no less than his natural happiness, either private or politic, man is *subject* : subject to the sovereignty of God, the Author of grace and nature, subject to the spiritual authority which is in the Church, subject to the temporal authority which is in the State.

Having laid down these principles, Leo XIII defines liberalism as the application to morals and politics of the claim to absolute independence which is the distinguishing characteristic in philosophy of rationalism and naturalism. It is therefore the refusal in practice to admit any control proceeding from anything other than ourselves.

He then proceeds to distinguish various degrees of this

[1] Leo XIII, encyclical *Libertas*.   [2] Cf. p. 68.

error : below absolute liberalism, which "rejects every authority and all divine law natural or supernatural,"[1] and refuses any kind of subjection " either in public life or private and domestic life,"[2] there is a liberalism of the second degree, which agrees to subject itself to the natural order, but refuses any kind of subjection to the supernatural. There is, finally, a third degree of liberalism which, accepting subjection to the supernatural order as far as individuals are concerned, refuses it as regards States.[3] It is clear, moreover, that, in virtue of the internal logic of the principle on which it is based, every form of liberalism tends to absolute liberalism as to its perfect type.

I do not propose to attempt a complete study of liberalism (that would require several volumes), but content myself in this note with a few observations on the subject.

(1) One liberal error makes the liberty of man consist in the independence of his will in regard to every exterior rule—this is " autonomy " in the Kantian sense, what Leo XIII calls *independent morality* ; or it would make the justice of social relations consist not in conformity to the divine law, but in the sole consent of individuals ; or again it would make liberty of thought consist in its independence in regard to reality, and the rejection of all constraint— a form of liberalism condemned by Gregory XVI in the Encyclical *Mirari vos* (15th August, 1832), when he recalled the question of St. Augustine : " Is there any worse death for a soul than liberty to go astray ? " (*Ep.* 166). Parity of truth and falsehood, of justice and injustice, of good and evil, is the metaphysical secret to which liberalism obscurely attunes the human soul.

(2) Another liberal error consists in denying the right of the spiritual power to intervene in temporal matters

---

[1] Cf. the Letter from the Secretariate of State to the Archbishop of Bogota.
[2] Encyclical *Libertas*.   [3] Letter to the Archbishop of Bogota.

ratione peccati, and the subordination of civil society to the Church of Christ because of the subordination of ends. This form of liberalism has been considered at length in the first chapter of this book.

(3) A third liberal error consists in denying that civil society has itself an end not only of a material but also of a moral order. This error is closely connected with the preceding one, for if civil society has not itself an end in the moral order, it does not of itself postulate—always presupposing the elevation of man to the supernatural order—its subordination to the society entrusted with the task of leading souls to the supreme supernatural end, and any such subordination would then be doing violence to civil society. This error is as categorically condemned by the teaching of Leo XIII as by St. Thomas Aquinas.[1] "Nature itself," says Leo XIII, "cries out that society ought to give the citizen the means and facility of living honourably, that is to say according to the laws of God. . . . Governments are strictly bound to take steps to secure, by the wisdom of their legislation, not only exterior advantages and benefits, but also and above all the welfare of the soul."[2]

"Man is born to live in society, for Providence has intended him, who cannot acquire in isolation either the resources necessary for the maintenance of life *or perfection of mind and heart*, to associate with his fellows in a society, not only domestic but also civil, which alone can procure perfect sufficiency of life, *vitae sufficientiam perfectam*."[3] "What is true of man, considered as an individual, is also true of society, both domestic and civil. Nature has not made society to be the last end of man, but so that man

---

[1] Some very explicit texts from St. Thomas Aquinas on this point will be found in the first chapter (pp. 11-12). Cf. also notes 20, 22 and 23.

[2] Leo XIII, Encyclical *Libertas*.

[3] Leo XIII, Encyclical *Immortale Dei* (1st November, 1885).

shall find in and through society the assistance he needs to attain his perfection. If a society, therefore, pursues exterior advantages, the elegance and abundance of the good things of life to the exclusion of everything else, if it professes to neglect God in the administration of the State and to take no account of moral laws, it is criminally deviating from its end and the commands of nature, it is not so much a society and human community as a fraudulent imitation and simulacrum of society." Then " force remains the sole guarantee of order and public tranquillity. But force is very weak indeed, if it is not based upon religion." [1]

It is, therefore, an error to consider, as is sometimes done, that the *temporal* common good, the end of the State, means an exclusively *material* good. It is both material and moral, but mainly moral : the upright life on this earth—in time—of the human multitude assembled in a social body.[2] But every man being ordered in the first place to an infinitely superior good, which is God, the supreme supernatural end of human life, the common good of the human State ought itself to be ordered to that supreme supernatural end ; and whereas the common

---

[1] Leo XIII, Encyclical *Sapientiae Christianae*.

[2] This common good. (*communicatio in bene vivendo*) is a different thing from the mere aggregation of particular goods, and is not the peculiar good of a whole which (like the species, for example, compared with individuals) relates only to itself and sacrifices the parts to itself ; it is the common good *of the whole and its parts*, a good which integrates particular goods in the whole so far as they are communicable (externally, in the natural manner of human communication here below), and as it is itself communicable to the parts—whether the material prosperity of the State be in question or its intellectual and moral patrimony. And this whole, not being a substantial whole, like a living organism, but a community of persons and families, ought to have regard for the more fundamental rights which natural law confers on human personality and domestic society. Otherwise it corrupts its own good.

Every individual, considered in his formal aspect as a constituent part of the State, is ordered to that common good of the State. But he is ordered in the first place, as a person destined for immortality, to God Himself, and on that score the State is but a means for him.

good of the State, being a *temporal* good, will cease with life on earth, the ultimate good, being eternal life, will never cease. This eternal and supernatural good, in which even in this life we participate through grace, this *spiritual* good (that is to say, it proceeds from union with the Holy Spirit) is the peculiar end of that divinely instituted society, superior to every human society, the Church, the mystic Body of Christ.

So we see that the Church alone, not the State, has jurisdiction over the spiritual, over what directly comes into contact with the salvation of souls and the worship of God—" the Church alone has been invested with such a power to govern souls, to the complete exclusion of the civil authority " [1]—and that, leading us to eternal life, she has a sovereign right of education and control over the moral life of man. But we also see that civil society can and ought to aim positively at procuring to the best of its power the virtuous life of the multitude : *to the best of its power*, that is to say on the one hand by legislating directly only in regard to exterior acts and itself making use only of exterior sanctions, and on the other hand by confining itself to the formal point of view of the common good of the social body, thereby defining very strictly the limits of its activity (and necessarily leaving room for the toleration of the lesser evil). Moreover, our moral activity being subordinated to the movement towards the last end, it is as instructed by the Church with regard to the things conducing to that end and in agreement with the Church (by acknowledging her direct power over the spiritual, her indirect power over the temporal) that the terrestrial State will conduce to the virtuous life. " Nature has not provided us with the means of mere existence, but of existence as moral beings. Therefore man expects from the tranquillity of public order, the immediate object of

[1] Leo XIII, Encyclical *Sapientiae Christianae*.

civil society, both the possibility of perfecting his existence and above all sufficient help to perfect his morals—a perfection which consists only in the knowledge and practice of virtue. At the same time he desires, as it is indeed his duty, to find in the Church such assistance as will enable him to acquit himself perfectly of his obligations to God : this is to be found in the knowledge and practice of true religion, which is the queen of the virtues, because by relating them to God, religion perfects and completes them all." [1]

(4) The peculiar end of civil society, therefore, is not only to secure respect for the individual liberties and rights of every citizen, or to ensure material comfort, but also to procure the truly human and therefore moral good of the social body. Liberty to practise any religion whatsoever indifferently [2] (as though the civil power were under no obligation, to the best of its ability and without claiming any jurisdiction over consciences, to do homage to truth), liberty to express any opinion, liberty to print anything,[3] liberty to teach any doctrine,[4] are all, therefore, even in the eyes of civil society, things contrary to nature.

[1] Leo XIII, Encyclical *Sapientiae Christianae*.

[2] *Syllabus*, Props. 78 and 79 (Denz.–Bannw., 1778 and 1779). Cf. the Encyclicals *Mirari vos, Immortale Dei* and *Libertas*. " Another liberty also loudly extolled," writes Leo XIII in the last-mentioned Encyclical, " is he liberty called freedom of conscience. If we are thereby given to understand that everyone is free to worship God or not as he likes, it is an error which the reasons given above are sufficient to refute. But it may also be understood in this sense that man in the State has the right to follow the will of God according to the dictates of his conscience and to fulfil His commandments, and that no hindrance should be offered to him. This true liberty, worthy of the children of God and gloriously protecting the dignity of human personality, is superior to all violence and oppression ; it is particularly dear to, and has always been desired by, the Church."

[3] Encyclicals *Mirari vos, Quanta cura* and *Libertas*.

[4] Cf. the Encyclical *Libertas* and the letter already quoted to the Archbishop of Bogota. " From such principles, which the Apostolic See has frequently condemned as false and contrary to Catholic doctrine, naturally flow as from a muddy spring the so-called modern liberties,

Either for the defence of the Church and the imprescriptible rights of the Church, or to direct itself properly
towards its peculiar end, the State has the right and the
duty to intervene in such matters, as it has the right and the
duty to see that justice is observed in private contracts.
The crime committed by many modern states is not
restraining such liberties (they constantly invoke them),
but restraining them *in an unjust and perverse way*, which is as
contrary to the law of God and the laws of the Church as
it is contrary to the moral good of man and the common
good of the State. The order is then completely reversed
in this sense that the temporal power, instead of legislating
in conformity with divine laws, of which the spiritual
power has charge, does so in contempt of those laws and
that power, and so turns things upside down.

Granted certain actual situations, " many people think
that the Church ought to move with the times, to accom-
modate and adapt herself to whatever the prudence of
the day may require in the government of societies. This
is an honourable opinion, if it be understood to refer to a
certain equitable manner of acting capable of being
reconciled with truth and justice, namely that the Church,
nursing the hope of some great good, should show some
complaisance and make whatever concessions she can to the
fashion of the day, while still preserving intact the sanctity
of her mission. But it is altogether different with such
practices and doctrines as the decline in morals and
erroneous opinions have illegally introduced. No age
can dispense with religion, truth and justice, high and holy

namely : liberty of worship, liberty of thought, liberty of teaching and
liberty of conscience." It is not to be thought that Catholic doctrine
claims to substitute in such spheres *constraint* or *servitude* for *liberty*.
It merely declares that the human being's liberty of action therein
ought to be regulated and defined. The objects of its condemnation
are liberties regarded as *inviolable* and considered as sovereign *rights* conferred on man by nature.

things which God has placed under the protection of the Church, and nothing could be more improper than to desire the Church to practise dissimulation in regard to error or injustice, or to connive at anything which might prove harmful to religion.

" It follows, therefore, from what has been said that it is in no way permissible to ask, to defend or to accord indiscriminate liberty of thought, of writing, of teaching, of religious worship, as so many rights bestowed on man by nature. For if nature had really bestowed them, it would be lawful to reject the sovereignty of God and no law could restrain human liberty.

" It also follows that such diverse sorts of liberties can for adequate reasons be tolerated, provided that an appropriate moderation prevents them from degenerating into licence and disorder.

" Lastly, wherever custom has established such liberties, the citizen must profit by them to do good and consider them in the same light as the Church. For every liberty must be accounted legitimate to the extent that it increases the power of doing good, and beyond that, never." [1]

The *thesis*, therefore (that is to say, the normal end in law to which one should always ideally refer and as far as possible tend), must be distinguished, as the current formula requires, from the *hypothesis* (that is to say, the aggregate of actual conditions determining *hic et nunc* the possibilities of realisation of the thesis).

From this last point of view the doctrine of St. Thomas on the various systems of political life may help us to form a better judgement of certain concrete cases. " Mixed systems " being according to him the best suited to human nature, St. Thomas distinguishes two principal forms of *mixed system*, the *monarchical* mixed system and the *republican*,

[1] Leo XIII, Encyclical *Libertas*.

which differ specifically by the way in which each conceives the common good.[1]

In the "perfect mixed system" (the best type of monarchy), which combines the monarchical principle (the rule of a single man entrusted with the unity of the whole) and the aristocratic principle (allocation of offices to those best fitted for them) and the democratic principle (participation by the masses in the administration of the State), the temporal common good is envisaged and directly aimed at in all its elevation, in its integrity of a political work (human, rational and moral) to be achieved, and presents itself formally as the *virtuous life of the multitude assembled in one*. Such a system, which commends itself from the point of view of *the greatest good*, is essentially constituted under the sign of *unity* and *value or virtue* ; the part played in the life of men therein by the orders of the public authority or government as such is considerable. Precisely because of its high ideal and the preponderance of solicitude for moral interests implicit in the definition of it, it cannot help controlling in a particularly firm manner the various liberties referred to in the documents just quoted : at the same time it invites the whole-hearted application of the principles which require the subordination of the temporal to the spiritual sovereignty : aiming positively at the "virtuous life," it must be positively subject to the control of the super-terrestrial State entrusted with the duty of leading man to his last end ; the indirect power, as in fact happened in the Middle Ages, will find many an opportunity for more or less imperative intervention.

The Republic (*politia*), which combines the democratic and oligarchical principles, is, in itself, according to St. Thomas (cf. *Comm. in Polit.*, iv, vii), a less perfect form

[1] Cf. Marcel Demongeot, *Le meilleur régime politique selon St. Thomas*, Paris, Blot, 1928.

of mixed system, the least elevated of the legitimate forms of political life. The temporal common good is there envisaged and aimed at in its least difficult, least positive aspect— merely as *procuring the greatest average convenience, the maximum general ease in the common life of men.* Such a system, which commends itself from the point of view of the *least evil*,[1] is essentially constituted under the sign of *political liberty ;* the part played in the life of men therein by government as such is weak. Without, therefore, excluding solicitude for moral interests, the preponderance of concern for excellent material functioning is implicit in the definition of it.

Such a political system will, therefore, hardly concern itself, and in proportion as its aims are the less elevated be as little concerned as possible, with regulating the various liberties before mentioned ; the radius of its activity will at the same time be the less likely to come into contact with the sphere of spiritual interests and come under the incidence of the power entrusted with the task of taking care of the salvation of souls ; and so long as such concrete conditions prevail, the Church may in fact find in liberty alone her

---

[1] Evil, in the philosophy of St. Thomas, being what most frequently happens in the human species, the point of view of the least evil in fact corresponds to what as a general rule succeeds best among the average of that unhappy species, especially if assistance derived from the supernatural order be left out of account. For this reason St. Thomas, who considered Monarchy to be the best of all political systems and the most desirable purely and simply, elsewhere writes : " If we do not mean the best system which can be desired and chosen purely and simply, but the best in fact attainable in the average of cases, we should say that a Republic and the mixed forms of aristocracy most closely approximating to it are the best systems which most States and men can realise " (in *Polit. Arist.*, iv, x, § 1)—systems which in fact are rarely realised, because it is their corrupt form which as a rule most frequently predominates (*ibid.*, § 16). We so perceive how the most intrinsically elevated political forms, which commend themselves from the point of view of the greatest good, stand in still greater need of the superior virtues which religion brings so as not to become corrupted among men, and how, in fact, Monarchy attains its perfect type in human society only if it is a *Christian monarchy.*

greatest chance of exercising influence. Such would seem to be the case at the present moment in the United States.[1]

If instead of having to deal with this normal type of *politia*, we have to deal with political forms concealing under the cloak of democracy principles and a spirit tending with religious fervour to set up a general state of materialism and atheism, the conditions would clearly be altogether different. Such systems would use the various liberties mentioned against God and man until such time as they were finally suppressed to the advantage of the all-powerful state. And the " hypothesis " would mean for the Church an aggregate of concrete conditions in which, whether she were patient and made the best of circumstances or resisted flagrant injustice, she would always have battles to fight.

(5) It is another liberal error to think that the source of civil power is not God, the Author of nature, but the masses, or even, as Rousseau said, that while its source is God, it *resides* in the masses, and that governments are mere delegates of the masses. The masses can, in certain forms of polity, appoint men to the task of watching over the public good, but, this appointment once made, sovereignty resides in them, not in the masses, and they hold it from on high, not from below. " Such a choice appoints the sovereign, but does not confer the rights of sovereignty. Authority is not thereby conferred : all that is determined is who shall exercise it." [2]

[1] The peculiar conditions prevailing in the United States explain how a mind, confining itself entirely *to the hypothesis* of the Constitution of that country, with no apparent awareness that the concrete circumstances so laid down may be theoretically conceived as non-existent, can produce in all sincerity so liberal a manifesto as that published in the *Atlantic Monthly* for May, 1927, by Mr. Alfred E. Smith in answer to the objections made to his candidature for the Presidency by Mr. Charles C. Marshall.

[2] Leo XIII, Encyclical *Diuturnum illud* (29th June, 1881). Cf. Pius IX, *Syllabus*, 60th proposition condemned : " Authority is merely the sum of numbers and material forces " ; Leo XIII, Encyclicals *Immortale Dei*, *Quod apostolici* and *Libertas* ; Pius X, Letter on the *Sillon*.

(6) It is still another liberal error to think that civil laws are not binding in conscience.[1] It is permissible to resist unjust laws, that is to say that, if a law is unjust because it enjoins something destructive of the good of the state,[2] it is not binding in conscience, " unless perhaps for the avoidance of scandal or commotion which the violation of it might entail ; for which reason man is bound to give up even his own right, as it is said in the Gospel of St. Matthew (v. 40, 41) : " *And if a man will contend with thee in judgement and take away thy coat, let go thy cloak also unto him. And whosoever will force thee one mile, go with him other two.*" [3] And if a law enjoins something contrary to the divine good, the commission of a sin or some act prohibited by natural or divine law, it must on no account be observed.[4] "But if the ordinances of legislation and princes," writes Leo XIII, " sanction or enjoin something contrary to divine or natural law, the dignity of the Christian name, duty and the apostolic precept alike proclaim that God must be obeyed before men." [5]

[1] The Thomist definition of law, recalled by Leo XIII (*Sapientiae Christianae*), is well known. Law is not the expression of Number or the General Will, " *but an order of the undeviating reason made by the lawful power with a view to the common good.*"

[2] E.g. when it violates a natural right of human personality or the family.

[3] St. Thomas Aquinas, *Sum. Theol.*, i–ii, 96, 4.

[4] St. Thomas Aquinas, *Sum. Theol.*, i–ii, 96, 4. May such resistance to unjust laws be attended by the use of force ? Cardinal Zigliara (*Summa philosophiae*, vol. iii ; *Jus naturae*, i–ii, c. 2, a. 7, § 17) answers in the affirmative, as regards occasions *of special gravity* and so far as *lawful self-defence* necessitates the use of force. The right of *passive resistance* would, he declares, be humanly ineffective, if it did not also involve the right of repelling by every honourable means (including force) acts of violence and aggression *effectively done* by the executive with a view to securing obedience to unjust laws. This the writer calls " defensive resistance," and the initiative in it must be taken by a lawful social authority.

[5] Leo XIII, *Quod apostolici*. Cf. *Diuturnum illud* ; *Sapientiae Christianae*. Conscience being the proximate guide of human actions, man must always act according to his conscience : if, then, the case should arise of an individual resisting a just law from motives of conscience—

But such exceptional cases apart, by the very fact that civil authority derives from God, men are bound in conscience to obey the laws of the State.[1] "It is no more permissible to condemn the lawful power in whomsoever it may reside than to oppose the will of God.[2] "Christians, therefore, invest the notion of authority with a religious veneration, for they see in it, even when it resides in an unworthy mandatory, a reflection and as it were an image of the Divine Majesty. They have the proper respect for law which law deserves, not because of force and penal sanctions, but in conscience bound, for *God has not given us a spirit of fear.*"[3]

I would add that an executive may enact unjust laws without on that account being necessarily unlawful.[4] An executive may not acknowledge that it derives its authority from God (thereby committing the most serious and grotesque error), without thereby necessarily losing that very authority which it derives from God although it denies it.

The laws which it enacts, so long as they prescribe nothing contrary to natural or divine law, continue to be binding in conscience. Gregory XVI (*Mirari vos*) and Leo XIII (*Diuturnum*), quoting St. Augustine, recall in this connection the attitude of the early Christians and the obedience they rendered to persecuting governments, even to such as Julian the Apostate.

because he believes that it commands him to commit a sin—he clearly incurs no guilt in following his conscience, but (except in case of invincible and absolutely involuntary error, even *in causa*) he is guilty of having a badly educated conscience at variance with the eternal law which is the first and supreme rule governing human actions. The public authority, therefore, if the law is just in itself, is within its rights in punishing his resistance by imposing on him the prescribed sanctions.

[1] St. Thomas Aquinas, *op. cit.*
[2] Leo XIII, *Immortale Dei.*
[3] Leo XIII, *Sapientiae Christianae.*
[4] Leo XIII distinguishing between the political régime and the legislation passed (Encyclical *In mediis*).

An authority becomes unlawful or tyrannical when it procures not the common good but the radical corruption of the common good. In such a case, according to St. Thomas,[1] it is the authority which, properly speaking, is seditious. It may then be lawful to overthrow it, unless a worse disorder would ensue and greater harm so befall the populace. In fact St. Thomas considers the risk of such worse disorder so considerable that in the *De Regimine Principum*[2] he leaves no other remedy, in a case in which a tyrant cannot be dethroned by the intervention of some superior authority, than recourse to Almighty God.[3] " If Princes should happen to proceed to rash excesses in the exercise of their authority," writes Leo XIII, " Catholic doctrine does not permit a spontaneous rebellion against them, for fear lest the tranquillity of order be more and more disturbed and society suffer still graver harm in consequence. And when the excesses have risen to such a pitch that all hope of salvation seems lost, it teaches that the remedy must be sought in the merits of Christian patience and urgent prayer to God."[4]

Nevertheless, it is clear that it is lawful to fight by every honourable means (that is not to say feeble means, because rebellion is not the only effective means, there are honourable means which are also energetic) a tyrannical or persecuting government (more particularly when it is engaged in sapping the very foundations of public good by the imposition of atheist teaching upon children or the

[1] *Sum. Theol.*, ii–ii, 42, 2.
[2] *De Regimine Principum*, i, 6.
[3] On the other hand, the reasons given by St. Thomas in the text from the *Summa* just quoted show—and recent examples (Russia on the one side, Hungary and Italy on the other) might be adduced in confirmation—that it may be the act of good citizens to take the place of failing authority once the latter abandons the State to revolution : for they are then rising up not against lawful authority but against sedition itself.

Leo XIII, Encyclical *Quod Apostolici*.

destruction of the natural organism of the family) ; or again to try to change by every honourable means for reasons of public interest the established régime. " When one is under the oppression or the menace of a tyranny overpowering the State under an unjust violence or seeking to deprive the Church of the liberty which is her due, one may lawfully seek another political organisation under which it may be possible to act with liberty. . . . Nor does the Church condemn the desire to free our country from either a foreigner or a despot, provided that such an end can be achieved without doing violence to justice." [1] " Let every man also retain the just and honourable liberty of preferring any particular form of government which is not at variance with the order of things established by Christ." [2]

(7) " Salvation, however, is not to be found elsewhere than in Christ : *for there is no other name under Heaven given to men in which we were to be saved.* It is therefore necessary to return to Him, to prostrate ourselves at His feet, to gather from His divine lips the words of eternal life ; for He alone can point the way to salvation, alone teach the truth, alone recall to life, Who said of Himself : *I am the Way, the Truth and the Life.* One more attempt has been made to deal with the affairs of the world without regard to Christ ; the building was begun by rejecting the cornerstone. Peter made the reproach to those who crucified Jesus. And once again the structure of the building has collapsed, breaking the heads of the builders. Jesus remains in spite of everything the corner-stone of human society, and once again the maxim is justified : There is no salvation but in Him." [3]

---

[1] Leo XIII, *Libertas.*
[2] Pius XI, Consistorial address of the 20th December, 1926.
[3] Pius X, *Jucunda sane.*

VI. DEMOCRATIC NATURALISM AND
ANTI-DEMOCRATIC NATURALISM

" Democracy, lawful in itself," Père Garrigou-Lagrange wrote recently, " may degenerate into democratism, into a kind of religion which confuses the order of grace and the order of nature or tends to reduce the supernatural truth of the Gospel to a social conception of human order, to transform divine charity into philanthropy, humanitarianism and liberalism. The Church may then intervene in virtue of her very magistracy. She cannot forget the maxim : *corruptio optimi pessima* ; the worst form of corruption is that which attacks what is best in us, the most exalted of the supernatural virtues, the soul of all the others. If there is nothing better in this world than true charity, which loves God above all things and its neighbour for the love of God, there is nothing worse than false charity, which reverses the very order of love, by making us forget the infinite goodness of God and His imprescriptible rights, to stuff our ears with the rights of man— equality, liberty and fraternity. The formal object of an essentially supernatural virtue so becomes confused with that of a feeling not unfrequently largely inspired by envy. Is that not the essence of the democracy-religion which completely falsifies the idea of the virtue of charity and at the same time that of virtue indissolubly bound with justice ? To seek to discover in it the spirit of the Gospel would be mere illuminism. To realise it, it is sufficient to apply the main rule for the discerning of spirits : ' The tree is judged by its fruits ' : the fruits produced by the works of Rousseau are not the fruits of the Gospel.

" To react properly against such democratism and those who profit by it to the great detriment of their country, is it sufficient to give the helm a vigorous turn in the opposite direction, in the human order ? Is it sufficient to recall the benefits conferred by the natural hierarchy of values once established by the guilds in the artisan world, the benefits conferred by an intellectual aristocracy and a landed aristocracy, the advantages derived from a monarchy which brought about unity and continuity in the home and foreign policy of a great country, to protect it against its enemies both within and without ? If such a reaction takes place only or mainly in the human order, and not sufficiently in the supernatural order of faith and love of God, it runs the risk of falling into the opposite extreme to that which it is fighting. Not only can it not effectively substitute, as it ought, for false notions of charity and justice the true conception of these virtues, but it can easily degenerate into an aristocratic naturalism recalling the wisdom of Greece and its intellectual pride in opposition to the spirit of the Gospel. The profound significance of the teaching of Our Lord respecting humility and love of our neighbour would be thenceforth lost : ' *I confess to thee, O Father, Lord of heaven and earth, because thou hast hid these things from the wise and prudent, and hast revealed them to little ones* ' (Matthew xi. 25). ' *This is my commandment, that you love one another, as I have loved you* ' (John xv. 12).

" To react against the naturalist conception of charity which is as it were the soul of democracy-religion, one must safeguard oneself against the opposite extreme which would be a contrary form of naturalism. One must rise above these two extremes to the culminating point which unites the theological and moral virtues, living faith, resolute hope, the supernatural love of God and our neighbour, of our very enemies, divine charity indissolubly bound to true justice. To rise to such a height, Christian humility is required ; it is a fundamental virtue and alone can repress the pride which tends to pervert every political conception and to warp every form of government. Humility must be accompanied by docility of the mind with regard to every natural and supernatural truth ; it is the only way to supreme truth and true wisdom " (Père Garrigou-Lagrange, *Vie Spirituelle*, March, 1927).

VII. THREE FORMS OF NATIONALISM

" Nationalism may be primarily understood : (*a*) in opposition to humanitarian myths, as the doctrine that the nation, considered as synonymous with the *civitas* or the country, is the highest *natural* social unity ; (*b*) in opposition to individualist errors, as the theory that the common good is ' more divine,' as Aristotle and St. Thomas say, than the individual good and different in kind from the mere aggregate of individual goods, and that the natural law (no less than the fourth commandment) bids us cherish the good of our country above our private interests. Nationalism may also be understood in the same sense in relation to the providential order as the doctrine that every nation has its own mission to fulfil in history and that these missions are not all identical. It is impossible not to approve of ' Nationalism ' in the primary sense, even if the threat of destruction against which it protects the patrimony of the country compels it to assume the appearance of a rather feverish reaction. It would no doubt be impossible to say purely and simply, even in face of exceptional circumstances, ' the national interest above all,' for God and the law of God always transcend the national interest (although it is none the less true that, the nation having a moral end, a real national interest requiring something contrary to the law of God would be a contradiction in terms : when St. Louis restored Guyenne to the King of England because justice required it, he was working in the true or metempirical interest of France). But the empirical criterion of national interest, which in the past has only too often come into criminal opposition with the laws of the Gospel, happens in fact, in the circumstances in which France is at present involved, to be particularly useful as a defence of the prime conditions of the restoration of order against the peril of general dissolution. I would add that to criticise liberal illusions in the name of the national interest is certainly legitimate, but that the criticisms need to be completed by pointing out the metaphysical and moral errors inherent in the principle of liberalism and to correct them every time they would seem to tend to a misconception of the authentic rights of conscience.

" Nationalism may be understood in a second sense as the systematic expression of the principle of nationalities carried to the extreme and is then more or less synonymous with *racialism:* So conceived, it is a very dangerous error. However desirable it may be to satisfy, in accordance with justice and in the heart of the civil unit, the aspirations of the various ' nations ' considered in the sense of *racial families*, the revolutionary dogma of the principle of nationalities (that unity of origin constitutes the *raison d'être* and unity of civil society and the members of each ethnic branch ought to assemble in so many nation-States) is a materialist illusion contrary to natural law and destructive of civilisation. Maurras, let it be said, has taken a definite stand against this interpretation of nationalism.

" There is finally a third sense of the word nationalism meaning the corrupt form of the legitimate nationalism as at first defined : it is then the blind worship of the nation (State or country), considered as transcending every moral and religious law, nationalism as opposed to God and the kingdom of God : as such it refuses to acknowledge the independence of the Church of Christ and her authority over temporal matters, an authority of the extent of which the Church is the sole judge in every case and which allows her to absolve the subjects of an apostate king of their oath of allegiance ; or it refuses to admit the liberty to preach the Gospel, claiming to subordinate it to the temporal interests of governments (as has so often happened in missionary countries) ; or it refuses to admit the duties of justice and charity of mutual obligation between nations, which forbid the making of war from mere desire for glory or lust of conquest or fomenting civil war in a neighbour's territory. It must be admitted that the love of State or country, by reason of its very nobility and disinterestedness, is such a powerful sentiment that without the superior control of a very vigorous supernatural spirit, it can easily incline *more or less* to such an excess. In the shape of Gallicanism, regalism and Josephism (continued and odiously aggravated by Jacobinism and State laicism, which refuses to admit the duties which the nation as such owes to God), it constituted the chief fault of the *ancien régime* before becoming a characteristic of the modern world ; Philip the Fair and some of his successors have from this point of view created a tradition, the moral of which it would be disastrous to adopt. If the word nationalism be understood in this third sense, one would have to be determinedly anti-nationalist.

" At a time when the world is rent by more fearful national antagonisms than ever, rendered not less violent but on the contrary still more dangerous by humanitarian illusions, spiritual Catholicity, at any rate, is still a living force, and what writer during the war laid greater stress upon it than Maurras ? It is in reliance upon it and by making in the first place an effort at comprehension in the supra-national domain of the spirit that an obedience *non fictum* should have been given to the exhortations which the Supreme Pontiffs have multiplied during these last years in favour of a permanent peace."

(*Une opinion sur Charles Maurras et le devoir des Catholiques*, pp. 66–72.)

VIII. ON CHINA

There are diseases which, transported to other climates and encountering organisms which have never been immunised, become deadly scourges. Marxism, transported into the Russian organism, produced Bolshevism. Europe rejected the kingship of Christ in its social life and thought that its apostasy was no great matter. That apostasy makes the round of the world, however, and returns to Europe with a scared face. The West is not satisfied with supplying the Chinese with arms and ammunition with which to kill one another [1]; everyone knows that it is the ulcers of its false philosophy which are at present corroding the Chinese mind and in China threatening the world.

" In China," Père Wiéger recently wrote in a remarkable article,[2] " in the years immediately preceding the Revolution which was felt to be imminent, more particularly after the establishment of the Republic, it was also *the Young* who went abroad, all hoping to become, like their Japan-

---

[1] " How do the big wigs come by these pretty toys, as a Prussian General called them, whose remark was repeated everywhere ? The answer is quite easy. They begin by extorting the money required from the people of China by threatening to cut their throats. They then pay the money into the outstretched palms of certain foreign contractors, who will deliver them arms and ammunition as often as they ask for them and for as many piastres as they are willing to pay. So the game can go on as long as there is any money left in China. Ah, Europeans, my brethren (I omit the Americans and the Japanese, who do not affect me so closely), nations which were said to have compassionate hearts . . . which moved the whole world to put an end to the slave trade, to suppress the traffic in alcohol and opium and are now providing the Chinese in abundance and with complaisance, with the means of massacring one another ! . . . Does the money you earn in such a way not burn your hands ? . . . If you were to stop feeding it, the civil war in China would stop immediately. ' It is you who keep it going' is the cry of the *Young Chinese*, and they are right. Sir Austen Chamberlain had to admit as much in the House of Commons on the 17th February, 1927 " (Père Léon Wiéger, " La Chine Actuelle," in *Études*, 5th April, 1927).

[2] *Études*, 5th April, 1927.

ese predecessors, members of the new aristocracy, stars in the new firmament. They studied, in Europe and America, politics and sociology, especially public education and national institutions. Less disciplined and of a more adventurous turn of mind than the Japanese (I am speaking of the Japanese of fifty years ago), they laid in a store of whatever would be useful to them in urging on the Revolution, advanced, subversive and extremist ideas, with which many schools, clubs and private individuals complacently supplied them.

" Such journeys and sojourns abroad were expensive, however, and not all the Young were able to travel. All, however, felt that they carried a revolutionary in their breasts. They were helped by a revolutionary change in official education. Elementary schools, lower and upper, secondary schools and academies on the new pattern were founded. A so-called National University and secondary school were set up in Peking to teach all that was most contagious in Europe, America and Japan. At the present moment, in the compulsory elementary schools, the descent of man from a monkey is being taught in its crudest form to children of from eight to twelve, the socialism of Marx and the communism of Lenin to pupils of from twelve to fifteen, in secondary schools the so-called scientific incredulity, and to undergraduates the atheism of Moscow according to the formula of Zinoviev : ' We shall in the end dethrone God in His heaven.' No more religion, morality, law, worship, parents or masters ! We want absolute liberty for everyone in everything, the abolition of every constraint and restriction ! Such is the cry of students of both sexes in China, for the spring of the *new learning* flows for boys and girls alike and the *new spirit* drives both equally mad.

" This power of propagation and contagion seems to me impossible to repress for reasons which I will explain and which deserve serious consideration, for they will determine the future.

" Public education has completely escaped the direction and even the control of the State. There is certainly in the Ministry at Peking a Minister of Education, but he is a mere ornament and has ceased to be of any practical importance. The public education of the entire country, North and South, is directed by two quasi-private and practically independent societies, the Federation of National Education and the Office for the development of Education. Each holds an annual congress. The latter lays down the general lines of policy. The former puts them into practice and draws up detailed programmes. Two enormous printing and publishing concerns *carry them out*, the Commercial Printing Company and the China Publishing Company, both established at Shanghai and with branches and agents everywhere. I have italicised the words ' *carry them out* ' for this reason. The most important thing is a text-book, which the master must content himself with explaining temperately, without superfluous comment, just enough for it to be understood. So in reality it is the author of the text-book, not the school-master, who does the teaching. . . .

" Now the two firms in question have drawn up in accordance with the new programmes and published two whole series of school manuals, one for the pupil and the other for the teacher. In practice there are only these two series and they are used in every school. Therefore, in the whole of China, that and that alone is taught by the schoolmasters word for word ; that and that alone is what the pupils learn like parrots. It is therefore easy to know what *Young China* has in its head and says, thinks and believes. Take the book of the elementary schoolmaster teaching the upper and lower classes and read it carefully. It is that and nothing else. Common everyday knowledge in reading, writing and arithmetic, geography, history and the natural sciences : in addition, for the infants, man's descent from a monkey : for older children, socialism and communism. The text-books for secondary schools teach the theory and practice of atheism, the inexistence of morality and law, the valuelessness of any principle. The citizen should be content with practising a sort of exterior civic decency, respect his neighbour's interests so as to protect his own, a rejuvenated form of Chinese ritualism, older than Confucius, as old as China itself. On the pretext of nationalism, the most absolute exclusivism, the most rabid xenophobia are inculcated. On the pretext of scientism, irreligion is made compulsory."

If only towards the end of the nineteenth century there had been a Chinese—a Chinese Catholic I mean, for none other could have succeeded in such an undertaking—to denounce to his fellow countrymen the danger latent in an apostate West ! It is very remarkable that such an invasion of Western atheism, scientism and socialism, capable of destroying very rapidly every *spiritual* and universally human element in the ancient culture of China, is also only capable—because merely *brutal* principles, essentially below the life of the spirit, are there involved—of isolating and exasperating into a hatred of one's neighbour all the *material* (in the Aristotelian sense of the word), strictly national and racial elements in that same culture. By a diabolical paradox, it is precisely in order to protect the rights of their own culture that the Chinese most intoxicated with the worst products of the West oppose Christianity at the present day. " That the Chinese are *civilised* people is undeniable. They were civilised even long before the Europeans and the Americans and they know it. It was they who civilised the Japanese and they have not forgotten it. Besides their civilisation, the Chinese have their own peculiar form of *culture*, which also is of venerable antiquity and very elevated. *A priori*, therefore, the pretence of *civilising*, of *cultivating*, them was doomed to failure and apt to infuriate them. Now it was the Japanese, the least competent in the eyes of the Chinese, who committed the blunder of proposing themselves as teachers of culture in 1923. This provoked a storm of anger which spread next to other nations, guilty of the same stupidity. It was the dread and horror of being *cultivated* by the foreigner against their will, of seeing their national culture ousted by a foreign culture, which first turned the Chinese against the Protestant schools, the American more especially, which formerly were highly esteemed. They turned out yellow Yankees ! The same fear, and this is worse, excited them next against Christianity, which formerly, if not admired, was at least tolerated or even respected. Modern Chinese teaching denying the transcendental character of religion and regarding it as an integral part of the peculiar culture of each nation, Christianity became detestable, as being the intrusion of a foreign culture. Young China hates it from this point of view, not because of its dogmas, and the anti-Christian League would exterminate it for the same reason." [1]

The truth is that Christianity alone—the grace of Christ which divinely perfects nature without destroying it—can maintain and preserve whatever *spiritual* treasures there may be in Chinese culture without injuring its *national and social individuality*, but elevating it in the service of God, Who is Spirit. It is the one hope which remains, as Père Lebbe has long insisted. Catholicism is by right the protector of the authentic culture of China and true Chinese patriotism—as of every genuine culture and every true patriotism.

The difficulty of forming an exact idea of China may be realised if we consider what sort of idea a learned Chinese

[1] Père Wiéger, *loc. cit.*

can form of Europe.[1]   We have the most valuable testimony in the experience of the missionaries to dispel our ignorance.   I cannot resist the temptation to reproduce here from the *Missions Catholiques* (18th March, 1927)[2] the admirable account given by Mgr. Guébriant, Superior of the Foreign Missions, in a lecture delivered in Lyons on the 16th February, 1927.

[1] Cf. e.g. Kou Houng Ming's book on *l'Esprit du peuple chinois* (Stock, 1927).

[2] Léopold Levaux's essay on *la Chine et les Missions* (Roseau d'Or, No. 10, 1926), since published as a pamphlet ; the *Bulletin de la jeunesse Catholique chinoise* (Louvain), Père Lebbe's pamphlet *Que sera la Chine demain ?* may all be usefully consulted, and, more generally, the publications devoted to the lore of the missions (*Xaveriana*) of the Jesuit College at Louvain, as well as the *Revue des Missions* published by the Benedictines of Saint André at Lophem, near Bruges.

[Reference should also be made to Pope Pius XI's Letter *Ab ipsis Pontificatus primordiis* dated the 15th June, 1926, addressed to the Prefects Apostolic of China " with reference to certain erroneous opinions concerning the work of the Church " in that country and first published in translation in the Sept.–Oct. numbers of *Le Bulletin des Missions*, 1928.

The erroneous opinions in question, widely prevalent, says the Pope, among the youth, chiefly consist in considering the activities of the Catholic Church in China as dictated solely by the unscrupulous ambitions of the various European governments and the zeal of the missionaries, therefore, as a covert form of political propaganda.

After referring to the *universal* character of the Catholic Church, which, in accordance with the precept in Matthew xxviii. 19, embraces all nations indifferently, the Pope declares that the task of evangelisation is not imposed upon the missionaries by their respective civil governments but by God Himself (John xv. 16), and that there is the testimony of history to prove that the Church has never failed in her duty to protect and assert the rights of nations against the arbitrary domination of kings and governments.   He then lays special stress on the urgent necessity of training a native clergy to take the place, as circumstances permit, of foreign missionaries and to parry the danger of an intemperate patriotism.   Titus and Timothy, foreigners though they were, preached the faith to the Cretans and the Ephesians ; Patrick, a Scot by birth, converted Ireland ; Boniface, a Breton, won the Germanies for Christ.   The Church accommodates herself to the exigencies of time and place, but her method is ever the same and her behest to her missionaries is to gather the native children and to educate them carefully in the hope that they may one day become priests.

The Pope concludes his letter with a prayer that the prejudices of the Chinese may be dissipated, their hostility to the Church disarmed and their great country restored to prosperity and peace.]

CHINA

" CHINA, the subject of my address to you this evening, is, in a way, my second country. I have spent thirty-six consecutive years of my life there—thirty-one in Sze-chwan the most remote province of the interior, and five in the famous province, more famous than ever to-day, whose capital is Canton. Between-whiles I have had to travel over nearly every other province of China making an apostolic visit, that is to say, a general investigation into the Missions, which the Holy See had requested me to undertake immediately after the War.

" I can therefore talk on China without failing in the respect due to my audience by talking on a subject I know nothing about. But, I hasten to add, such knowledge as I possess of that great country is not in the least scientific. I have seen it, resided in it, become familiar with it during many years : I have, so to speak, lived it : I have compared my experiences and my impressions with those of my colleagues, missionaries from all countries and establishments. But I have not made any special study of China and Chinese questions. I have scarcely read anything at all, for, in my long lifetime as a missionary, I had no books and now, in my office of Superior of the Foreign Missions, I have no time.

" Having said so much and with the assurance that you will not attach to my remarks an importance which they do not possess, I will put before you very simply and very willingly my views on China and what is happening there at the present moment.

" China is the greatest country in the world, the most populous, the most compact, the richest in possibilities of every kind and possessing everything necessary to become the most powerful.

" Do you think that an overstatement? Consider, if you please, the attitude of the great powers with regard to China in revolution. They still call themselves the great powers, but what a tremendous contrast between words and facts ! One of them has done nothing but hesitate for the last two years or begun to pack up. It allows its trade to be boycotted, its concessions to be invaded, its nationals to be threatened, and all this time the other powers, less obviously aimed at, are only the more discreet in their expectations. Why ? Clearly because they are afraid, afraid of China, not as it is at the moment, but as it may reveal itself at any time, if it succeeds in organising itself, for it would then be a formidable power and no nation desires to give such a power the slightest excuse for turning against it when the time comes.

" What constitutes the power of China is not so much the extent of its territory or the riches of its soil or subsoil, as the qualities of the race which inhabits it ; an abundantly prolific race eager to live. Wherever it discharges its superfluity, it adapts itself to all climates and environments without losing its peculiar character and brings to the struggle for life an unrivalled perseverance and energy. The fertility of the Chinese population is a brutal fact which strikes the eye at once. I should hesitate to say that the increase of population in China itself is very fast. Children, it is true, are born in prodigious numbers, but they die in frightful proportions and, besides, the rate of mortality in general is very high in such a swarming population. There are no official statistics which enable one to give exact figures, but I have the impression, confirmed by my missionary colleagues, that the numbers in our Christian communities, where well-kept registers make it possible to keep an accurate check, would be stationary, or nearly so, if not increased by conversions.

"Now what is true of Christian communities can only be true *a fortiori* of the pagan mass. The reason is over-population, the lack of hygiene and cleanliness, the frequent famines and other causes, such as the suppression of little girls.

"There is indeed an interior emigration whereby over-populated cantons flow over into less inhabited or even quite uninhabited areas, for such there still are. But the indifference of the administration, which takes no interest in such questions and does nothing to encourage, guide and support the emigrants, derives no advantage from such social movements, and the emigrants, left to their own devices, are exposed to every hardship and disappear in large numbers without leaving any trace.

"This is not true, however, of Manchuria, a country of fertile steppes which only need strong arms to provide the richest harvests.

"Owing to its proximity to the over-populated agricultural provinces of the North, to Shan-tung especially, it attracted colonists in the end and the first colonists attracted others, so that solely through the energy of its admirable people, the Chinese republic has been increased by new provinces, with a population, approximately, of at least twenty million inhabitants. The same thing could happen, and for the same reason, in Mongolia. What would the results be if a strong and intelligent government, instead of living from day to day only more or less acknowledged by the nation, systematically took in hand a colonisation for which it has all the cards in its hand : an enormous fertile country, a prolific and laborious population ?

"What cannot be absorbed by interior colonisation naturally seeks an outlet abroad. But whereas the Chinese of the North turn their eyes to Manchuria, Mongolia and even Siberia, the Cantonese emigrate abroad. I say 'Cantonese' advisedly and not Southern Chinese, because I have never had the impression that there are two Chinas, one in the North and the other in the South, whereas the difference between China, properly so called, and Cantonese China is immediately perceptible. Only I understand the term Cantonese China in a very comprehensive sense which includes not only the province of Canton but Fu-kien as well, embraces to however small an extent neighbouring provinces and makes no distinction between the three human branches—I hardly venture to say the three races—inhabiting the country, the Cantonese properly so called (or Punti), the Hakka and the Hokklo. Now it is a remarkable fact, a fact, I fancy, not very well known—it escaped my own notice during my thirty years' residence in Sze-chwan, before I was transferred to Canton —it is a remarkable fact, I repeat, that Chinese emigration abroad has been up to the present exclusively Cantonese, Hakka, Hokklo or Fu-kiennese.

"The Northern Chinese, also, no doubt have begun to travel : students especially, for Northern Chinese are to be encountered pretty well everywhere in the world. But they never establish themselves outside their own country. They have no colonies anywhere, to my knowledge, except in Siberia. The Cantonese, on the other hand, of every kind and the Fu-kiennese spread everywhere and anywhere a door is open. Go and inquire in Indo-China or Malaya, the Straits Settlements or Java, the Philippines or New Guinea, in South America or the United States, the Antilles, Peru, even South Africa, the Transvaal, Mauritius or Reunion Island, all the Chinese you will find established there, either settled definitely in the country and taking root or spending the whole or only part of their lives there, busily engaged in trade or on the plantations, all these Chinese, I say, are Cantonese or Fu-kiennese, speaking one or other of the dialects of Southern China which other Chinese do not understand.

" Whatever the significance of such an observation, it is clear that China, both North and South, is a formidable reservoir of men, and whoever has seen it close-up cannot rid himself of the feeling that some phenomenon or other is preparing there of the same sort as the flood, unless it be a tidal wave.

" Because—and this is the second characteristic which strikes me most in regard to the Chinese—they have a marvellous facility of adapting themselves to all climates and environments. The Japanese seem to be a long way their inferiors in this respect. One would say that they cannot adapt themselves to the heat of the tropics or to the severe cold of the high latitudes ; there is, therefore, no Japanese colonisation of Formosa and yet the Mikado has been sovereign there for the last thirty years ; and, as for cold countries, it is only with difficulty, slowly and painfully, that the Japanese succeed in populating the great island of Hokkaido or Yezo, the most northern of their own archipelago. How much greater is the adaptability of the Chinese ! It is true that their country, which is as large as Europe, offers the greatest diversity of climate from the borders of Siberia down to such low latitudes as that of Tonkin. And the Chinese prosper in every country in which they have been allowed to settle. In the whole peninsula of Indo-China, they adapt themselves to the French, English and Siamese administrations indifferently and are already to be reckoned in millions : there are millions of them, also, in the Dutch Indies, hundreds of thousands in Eastern Siberia. And yet, where, I ask you, where can a more violent physical contrast be found than between the climate of Batavia and that of Baikal, a greater moral contrast than between the administration of an English colony and that of a Russian Soviet Republic ?

" Here another quality of the Chinese race comes into play, the third of those which I consider most character-istic . . . its energy, I would go so far as to say its fury, in the struggle for life. Canton, the great metropolis of Eastern Asia, with its violent psychology, Canton with its four or five million inhabitants, in city and suburbs, is perhaps the best place to choose in which to observe the intensity of the Chinese will to live. I had been transferred there by the order of Pope Benedict XV, after spending thirty-one years in Sze-chwan, and the change had cost me a lot. In the beginning, the population of Canton struck me as horrible : it was such a violent contrast to the laborious but tranquil simplicity of the peasants of my beloved province. Well ! I came in the end to find some-thing beautiful in all that squalor. And that something beautiful was precisely the courage with which that innumerable population struggles for a livelihood, from the old woman of eighty still rowing in the sampans down to the urchin of ten selling pastry cooked with rancid oil. Such an effort, bitterly, but on the whole honestly, main-tained to overcome the difficulty of living in the midst of such fierce competition, such an effort, by its intensity and perseverance, becomes a beautiful thing to see, and I came to admire it sincerely and love it with my whole heart. Now what is true of Canton is true everywhere else in China, even where local circumstances require not so much variety and ingenuity of effort. The Chinese people is in the highest degree a laborious people.

" I would add that it is also temperate—everybody knows that—and, lastly, that it is one, a unity imperilled by no separatist movement. The Cantonese and the Northerns fight each other, but both alike profess to be purely and simply China, the China which neither could conceive

otherwise than as the compact mass of Chung-kwei, the
' Nation of the Middle.'

" Is it not true that China, so considered, an enormous
superficial area, a dense population, ceaselessly multi-
plying, a unit for thousands of years past and conscious of
its unity, constitutes a singularly imposing force, and that its
near future appears as one of the most troublesome among
the many harassing problems before us ?

" The Catholic missionaries are not to blame if the terms
of the problem now present themselves in all their acuteness.
The object of their effort for centuries past to Christianise
China was first and foremost the welfare of the Chinese.
But they were none the less aware of the danger which their
evangelical work, if it had attained its object, would have
spared the world. Their dream was to see the people of
the Far East assimilate the essentials of our Chr'stian
civilisation and perfect it still further by adapting thereto
every good thing they themselves derived from their own
past. That would have meant their expansion in liberty,
justice and peace, to the advantage of the general progress
of humanity.

" Christianity, unfortunately, long confined to the cata-
combs by the mistrust of governments, then distorted by
parasitical propaganda, finally thwarted, if not discredited,
by the example of Christians themselves, was accepted
only by a few. And what it might have procured for the
people without upheaval or violence, they now want to
conquer without it and by force.

" No, it is not the fault of the missionaries or of Catholic
France. When one thinks of St. Louis sending religious
as ambassadors to the potentates of the East, of the French
Pope, Clement V, dispatching bishops to China in the
early years of the fourteenth century, of the Society for
Foreign Missions issuing in the seventeenth century from the
generous impulses of the French clergy, anxious to provide

the newly-established Christian communities of the Far East with priests of their own race, of Pauline Jaricot organising at Lyons a hundred years ago the Congregation for the Propagation of the Faith, of Mgr. de Forbin-Janson establishing that of the Holy Childhood ; when one sees that the more recent Congregation of St. Peter the Apostle, in which the Holy See reposes such high hopes for a native clergy, is also a French promotion, one is entitled to say that French hands were the first to be held out and have never ceased to be held out, in an absolutely religious and therefore entirely disinterested intention, towards those whom modern rhetoric has at last begun to describe, but not without a degree of pomposity, as ' our coloured brethren.'

" Be that as it may, China now presents a formidable problem, of which the data would appear to be as follows.

" The present unrest in China—it seems to me undeniable—is a nationalist impulse. To attempt to explain it by considering it as xenophobia pure and simple would be neither right nor prudent. It is easy, no doubt, to perceive in such an upheaval the resurrection of ancient hatreds and an unjustified contempt for the foreigner, and incidents have already occurred which later will make the Chinese blush. But what, as a matter of fact, they want to wrest from the foreigner is a hegemony which has long been a fact without, however, having become a right. Now that is legitimate. A great people is not wrong in wanting to be free and respected, master in its own house, to deal with other nations on a footing of equality, and to be the first to profit by its own riches.

" Such an aspiration has been consciously felt only for a few years, a generation at the outside. It made its first appearance among the young students, when they saw that the age-old illusion which confused China in the mind of the educated with the world and the world with China had vanished once and for all. For there was not even a precise word to distinguish the two : *Thien hia*, ' Under the sky,' applied equally to both.

" Once the idea of autonomous nations independent of the Son of the Sky was accepted, once their power and nature came to be understood and the character of their relations with China analysed, the irregularities, excesses, brutalities, and the injustices in the attitude adopted by the white nations with regard to China were perceived with evidence which became clearer and clearer. There is no better explanation of the pitch to which discontent grew, once such discoveries were made, and its present nature, than the title of the ultra-modern newspaper which is most popular in Shanghai, *Sin sze*, ' The lion awake.'

" In truth, the blindness of the Imperial Chinese Government was most to blame of all. Instead of abandoning once and for all its old foolish fancies and entering into normal relations with foreigners, it preferred to gain time by playing a card which it used for long with professional skill : pitting rival interests against one another. But that could not last for ever, and such time as it gained for the Government was time irrecoverably lost for China.

" I deeply regret it, and I am convinced that many of China's best friends regret it as much as I do. For the situation would be very different from what it is at the moment if the Imperial Government had opened its eyes a few years earlier. The Boxer Rising (1900–1901) and its severe lessons were required to convince it. Then, under the famous Empress Dowager Tse Hi and the regency which followed her disappearance, came a fruitful period during which every hope might be legitimately entertained. Necessary reforms, even such as ancient China had not foreseen, were made one after another, without shock or revolution, thanks to the survival of the traditional authority which was everywhere acknowledged and obeyed. We who were then living in China, had the strong impression that the great Empire had at last found its feet and that, after the lapse of a few years, without revolution or catastrophe, without breaking with its past, having become quite naturally master of its destiny, powerful among the most powerful States, it would see the inequalities of which it complained spontaneously disappear, with nobody in the whole world left before it but friends or customers eager to dispute its favour.

" Less than twenty years would have sufficed : but that was too long. Young China had had time to educate itself : it could not wait. It had received its education where it could, in the countless schools and universities of the Protestant missions or abroad, more particularly in Japan and the U.S.A. It had not yet discovered, as it since has, the masters of revolution in France. I need not dwell on the point, but I should like to emphasise one undeniable fact : the young people I am talking about were not the product of the Catholic schools.

" Here you will allow me perhaps to open a parenthesis and to explain to you why the Chinese youth, which is in such a state of effervescence to-day, has received only the smallest fraction of the education given in the Catholic schools or Catholic training. It was certainly not averse from such education : it has given ample proof of its liking for it in the last twenty-five years. Wherever we have been able to provide it with teachers, it has not only shown confidence in them, but, I think I may say so, a genuine preference. This is true not only of China, but also of Japan, Indo-China and Siam. . . . Now how many schools have we been able to open for children in the Far East ? Very much less than a tenth of those required from us. For every one which they have filled and in which they fight for places, we should have had twenty.

"Why? You have nothing to learn from me. At the very moment when the rush of Chinese youth to the new teaching was at its height, the French laws with which you are familiar had had time to destroy the French teaching staff from which the Catholic missions might have derived an incalculable advantage. In 1901, I had secured for my dear province of Sze-chwan the precious services of a teaching community very well known in Lyons, the Marist Brothers. Three schools were opened. We had a fine start, for the movement which we foresaw had not yet begun. Our schools made a humble beginning : but it was a beginning, and there was no doubt about the future. But after a few years, when what had been foreseen actually happened, the novitiate at Saint-Genis-Laval was closed and its excellent teachers dispersed. The same thing happened with regard to every congregation which might have provided French missionaries with the staff they required. May associations such as the *Amis des Missions* play their part effectively and help to save our France in the future from the error of a policy which has withdrawn hundreds of thousands of young people from the educative influence of French missionaries, with the result that in Africa ten million fetish-worshippers have become Mohammedans instead of becoming Christians, and out of eighteen million Annamites there are only a million and a half Christians, when there could easily be three times as many !

"But to return to young China. . . . So it had to have a revolution. It had it in 1911. And ever since then, the slow but certain development, which had been taking place gradually for nearly ten years, was succeeded by an era of confusion, trouble and warfare which continues until the present day.

"Shall we soon see the end of it? It may be so, but in what form ?

"The policy pursued by the powers in regard to China has, it must be confessed, been nearly always, but more especially since the revolution of 1911, a policy of selfishness. Selfishness is not an earnest of happiness. Each of them has attempted to secure the greatest share of profit in exploiting a market the like of which is nowhere to be found. Everything was thought of except the Chinese nation. It sought to find some support in order to realise its aspirations. Nobody dreamed of offering it any. Only one hand was outstretched to find it in the darkness, and by dint of supple patience in the end clasped it. With undeniable cunning it gave up groping in the North and came to set fire in the South, where it felt the tinder lay. Canton, the famous Canton, raised the red flag. The slogan for the time being is ' Down with Imperialism ! ' Those who recite it parrot-wise—and nowadays it is every Chinese—scarcely realise what it conceals. They will soon. What is certain is that the Bolshevist prescription has proved its efficacy. The Russian experiment is there to show its truly sovereign virtue when it is a question of repudiating treaties and destroying credit. That is all that is required to begin with. Later we shall see. The prescription is excellent for use abroad, but may perhaps be worthless for home consumption : once again, we shall see. And if necessary, a change will be made. But in the meantime, ' Down with the English,' with the support of our Russian friends. The rest will follow.

"There is something to be said for the argument. But it contains the most formidable elements of the unknown. It will always be time enough to reject the Muscovite prescriptions when they have yielded every advantage they contain. That is what they say, what is in everyone's mind. And, I am convinced, in absolute good faith. But will there always really be time to repent, to make a fresh start ? That I do not believe. And the Russian experiment is not alone to prove that social movements, once launched on their career, are not to be stopped where one likes. There is never a lack of extreme elements to shout ' On, On ! ' And on they must go.

" I leave you to draw whatever conclusion you think best. For my own part I would end on an optimistic note. We know that, whatever happens, we must never despair of the French. I will say that, whatever happens, we must never despair of the Chinese either. That nation wants above all to live. I said so in the beginning. And one of its chief qualities is common sense. It will not allow itself to be deceived and take for a formula of life what is a formula of death. Let us preserve the esteem and sympathy and confidence we have for it. And let us be prepared for the day when our disinterested support may be useful to it."

" It is not generally realised," said Pope Pius XI
recently, " what valuable, excellent and profoundly
Christian elements still remain in fragments of the ancient
Catholic faith. Boulders loosened from an auriferous
rock are also auriferous. The venerable forms of Eastern
Christianity retain such sanctity in their objects that they
deserve not only respect but also sympathy " (Address to
the Italian University Federation, *Osservatore Romano*,
10th and 11th, and 26th January, 1927, quoted in
Irenikon).

Few incidents in the history of the world have been
pregnant with such a mysterious and tragic importance
as the spiritual ordeal now being undergone by Russia and
the Russian Church. If the Bolshevist revolution, which
is essentially aimed *against God*, is a precursory sign of
the Man of Sin, may not the vast movement of faith aroused
in the Russian Church, so much suffering, so much blood,
so many martyrs and such heroic testimony, herald and
prepare the way for some great work of Christ and the
Holy Ghost ? It is not for nothing that Providence has
dispersed throughout Europe such numbers of Russian
exiles from their country and a whole youth eager for a
renewal of religion. We should meet them in the name
of Christ and with the love of Christ, so as to *make each
other's acquaintance* in Him and help one another to piece
together again, in our own selves in the first place, all
that has been shattered. Leaving out of account the
internal difficulties which may afflict Orthodoxy itself
in a land of emigration, I am well aware of all the obstacles
in the way of unity, the prejudices and stupidities which

each side may allege against the other, the violent and unjust animosity which inspires many Orthodox theologians against the Catholic Church, more particularly the danger of subjecting the spiritual to the national and political latent in such theories as Eurasianism. There is only one Church of which Christ Himself is Head with the Pope for Vicar on earth : whatever current of divine grace circulates in the separated churches of Christendom binds them invisibly (*voto*) to that one Church : but that virtual attachment must be realised in the exterior unity of dogma and the supreme spiritual government, which will not be achieved without many difficulties. God, however, does not inspire His children's hearts with certain profound aspirations to leave them ever unsatisfied. However tedious and prolonged the work He desires may be, obscure efforts made here and there, in the simplicity of the spirit of the Gospel, with a view to a more thorough and fraternal reciprocal understanding, will not remain without fruit.

The Western public is unfamiliar with Russian speculative thought. It has only just heard the names of such as Khomiakoff, Soloviev and Berdiaeff. Theology, mysticism and philosophy have, as a rule, been the main preoccupations of Russian speculation without distinction. It would, however, appear that there is a desire stirring at the present time in the intellectual youth of Russia, which is acutely conscious of the criteriological problem, for a *philosophy* in the proper sense of the term. The phenomenon is not without importance, and it is desirable that Catholics, and the disciples of St. Thomas especially, should show an appropriate interest. Their task would be, more particularly, to show the Orthodox how completely the Catholic conception of nature and grace, and the Thomist idea of a human nature, which is not closed, as the Stoics thought, but *open* and *perfectible*—and in fact made perfect and super-elevated by grace—are in harmony

176

with the genuine requirements of the Christian spirit no less than with those of philosophy.

The more deeply one considers such questions, the more clearly one perceives that the chief obstacle to union lies in a misunderstanding, a confusion between the *spiritual temperament* and the culture of one or other and *the Church* which is universal. The spirit of Orthodoxy is not the same thing as the Russian spirit ; the spirit of Catholicism is not the same thing as the Latin spirit. Once these things are well and truly realised on both sides, unity will not be far to seek. The most genuine and irreducible differences (they are to be found everywhere : " The East," said Mgr. Szepticky, " differs from the West even in questions where there is no difference at all ") are legitimate differences, and they ought to remain : differences not only in rite, but also and above all in psychology and spirituality. If due proportion be observed, such differences no more prevent unity in faith and discipline than differences in the West between, e.g., Benedictine and Franciscan spirituality. And besides, the nearer they get to God, the closer are souls brought together. In teaching that the object of Christian life is the acquisition of the Holy Ghost, a *staretz* such as Seraphim is inculcating the same doctrine as a St. John of the Cross, and they are both preaching the same doctrine as St. Paul. The best, the most urgent way of knowing one another, is for Orthodox and Catholic to know and to love one another in the most saintly representatives of their spirituality.

I was pleased to find some of these points of view in an article on *The Spirit of Orthodoxy* published by Père Tsébricov, a deacon of the Orthodox Church, in the periodical *Irenikon*.[1]

[1] I would draw the attention of persons interested in such questions to this most instructive review published by the Benedictines of Amay-sur-Meuse in Belgium, and also to two pamphlets by Père Woroniecki. The number I quote from (No. 7) also contains a summary biblio-

" To get to know Catholicism," he writes, " it is saints such as St. Francis of Assisi and the Curé d'Ars whom we Orthodox should consider. To get to know Orthodoxy, Western Catholicism should study with love and care its genuine initiates. . . .

" The very prevalent idea amongst Russians is that union with Catholicism means at bottom a spiritual and material *domination* by Rome, a foreign domination which would involve *denationalisation* and the loss of their individuality : that is the origin of the animosity which persists in the mass of the faithful.

" Nevertheless, the admission that such is the point of view of the Orthodox Church, even though many of its dignitaries should be found to share it, would be another gross confusion of the spiritual and the psychological provinces.

" Consequently, it might be said that the spirit of hostility to Catholicism is the result of a tragic misunderstanding, the source of which is not of a religious nature. . . .

" To sum up, I would say that it is not so much the idea of reunion among the Churches which can attract Eastern minds, as that of creating an atmosphere of understanding and charity, so as to make room for the spirit of God, which will be the sole author of unity. And it must be said that the tendency towards union ought to be envisaged from this point of view, if it is to find adherents among the Orthodox. A definite distinction must be drawn between Christ and His Kingdom and the Latin, German, Greek and Slav spirit, all problems must be transported into the heavenly region, and it should never be forgotten

graphy of the chief works which may be usefully consulted on the subject of Russian Orthodoxy and the Eastern Churches. Père Woroniecki's pamphlets are entitled *Les malheurs de la Russie* and *Le Catholicisme et l'Avenir de la Russie*. The latter first appeared in *Études religieuses*, Liége, 10th November, 1926.

that the most characteristic feature of Orthodoxy and, I believe, of all Christianity, is the strongly rooted idea that 'We have not here a lasting city, but we seek one that is to come' (Hebrews xiii. 14).

" That is all very well, it may perhaps be objected, but with that spirit you appear to forget the fact of the dogmatic differences dividing the Churches ! You can create whatever atmosphere you please, but at any given moment all the dogmatic quarrels will emerge. . . .

" Such an objection—I would answer—argues a lack of faith in God and His power. What men find impossible is possible for God. But for God to come and act in our midst, we must be worthy of His presence."

Before coming, as it will be necessary to some day, to the question of these dogmatic differences and the question of unity of government and jurisdiction essential to the unity of the mystic Body of Christ,[1] it is necessary—and the aspirations of Père Tsébricov in this respect agree with those to which Pius XI has given such frequent expression —to work in the first place for reciprocal understanding and acquaintance in an atmosphere of intelligence and charity. The spirit of God will do the rest.

" In this matter," the Pope writes, " it is important that the Eastern Dissenters, on the one hand, should give up their ancient prejudices and strive to become acquainted with the true life of the Church, and not blame her for the mistakes of individuals which the Church condemns and endeavours to set right : and that the Latins, on the other hand, should inform themselves more generously and profoundly of Eastern practices and customs, bearing

---

[1] Cf. Vladimir Soloviev's admirable book *La Russie et l'Église universelle*. Soloviev was of opinion that, as a result of historical circumstances, the Russian Church, although separated from the Catholic Church *de facto*, unlike the Patriarchate of Constantinople, was not separated from it *de jure*. (Cf. also Dom Lev Gillet's article in *Irenikon*, No. 1, April, 1926.)

in mind the advantage which St. Josaphat derived from such knowledge.

" This is the reason which determined Us to give a fresh impulse to the Pontifical Oriental Institute founded by Our greatly regretted predecessor Benedict XV ; for We are convinced that a more complete knowledge will not fail to widen mutual esteem and sympathy, and that these, combined with charity, will by the grace of God very effectively serve the cause of unity" (Encyclical *Ecclesiam Dei*, on St. Josaphat, 12th November, 1923).[1]

" We firmly hope that the pious resolutions of such Congresses will powerfully assist in dissipating many doubts and errors, often of a monstrous sort, which have taken root in the public mind with regard to everything affecting the history and religious life of the East" (Letter of the 21st June, 1924, to Mgr. Precan, Archbishop of Olomucz, with reference to the Congress of Velehrad which periodically brings together Catholic specialists in Eastern questions and Orthodox professors and men of learning from Slav and Eastern countries).

" The work of reconciliation," said Pius XI again, " can be attempted with a firm hope of success only on three conditions ; we must rid ourselves of current errors accumulated in the course of centuries with regard to the beliefs and institutions of the Oriental Churches. The Easterns, on the other hand, must devote themselves to considering the identity of teaching of the Greek and Latin Fathers. Thirdly, there must be an exchange of views between both sides in a high spirit of charity" (Consistorial Address of the 18th December, 1924, quoted in *Irenikon*, No. 1, April, 1926).

[1] On the occasion of the third centenary of his martyrdom. St. Josaphat was Archbishop of Polotsk and of the Oriental Rite.

NOTES

[1] Père Humbert Clérissac, *Le Mystère de l'Église*, 3rd ed., Saint-Maximin, 1925. This book should be read or re-read, as well as Joseph de Maistre's two books *Du Pape* and *L'Eglise Gallicane*. On the honours paid to the Christian Emperors, cf. Batiffol-Bréhier, *Les survivances du culte impérial*.

[2] A similar distinction is drawn in certain Scholastic text-books between the *jus naturae individuale*, the *jus naturae sociale*, and *ethica generalis*—law (private or social), which considers one's actions in relation to an intermediate end (other men considered as individuals or as constituting a social whole), thus being, as opposed to Kant's theory, subordinated to morality and part of it, morality considering our actions in relation to the ultimate end. (Cf. Gredt, *Elementa philosophiae aristotelico-thomisticae*, 3rd ed., vol. ii, No. 826.)

[3] So also they had no clear knowledge of creation. There is a striking analogy here. As they never succeeded in liberating the divine action completely from matter, so they never succeeded in liberating ethics completely from politics.

[4] *Imitation*, iii, 31.

[5] *Une opinion sur Charles Maurras et le devoir des Catholiques*, pp. 30-31.

[6] Cf. John of St. Thomas, *Curs. Theol.*, disp. xxii, a. 3 (vol. iv in Vivès edition).

[7] " The mystic Body of the Church consists not only of
181

men but also of angels : but the head of the whole multi-tude is Christ." St. Thomas, *Sum. Theol.*, iii, 8, 4.

[8] Étienne de Tournai. Cf. Gierke, *Political Theories of the Middle Ages*, translated with introduction by F. W. Maitland ; Carlyle, R. W. and A. J., *A History of Mediæval Political Theory in the West* ; G. de Lagarde, *Recherches sur l'esprit politique de la Réforme* ; Jean Rivière, *Le Problème de l'Église et de l'État au temps de Philippe le Bel.*

[9] " There are two things by which this world is chiefly governed : the sacred authority of the pontiffs and the power of kings. In which the burden of the priests is all the heavier, inasmuch as they will have to render an account to the Lord for the conduct of kings as well as for their own." (Letter of St. Gelasius I to the Emperor Anastasius, A.D. 494. Migne, PL, lix, 42, A.)

[10] Leo XIII, Encyclical *Immortale Dei.* Cf. the Encyclical *Sapientiae Christianae* : " The limits of rights and duties once and for all defined, it is abundantly clear that rulers of States are free to administer their own affairs and that not only with the passive toleration of the Church but plainly with her active co-operation. . . . Church and State have each its own province in which each is supreme : therefore neither owes obedience to the other in the administration of its own affairs within the boundaries appointed to each."

[11] " States cannot, without committing a crime, so conduct themselves as though God were utterly non-existent or refuse to take any interest in religion as some-thing exotic and profitless, or adopt from various kinds indifferently whatever they choose ; they have an absolute duty to follow the use and custom of worship according to which God Himself has revealed His desire to be wor-

shipped " (Leo XIII, Encyclical *Immortale Dei*, 1st November, 1885).

[12] Cf. Pope Pius XI, Encyclical *Quas Primas* : " He would be guilty of a disgraceful error who denied the authority of the Man-Christ over any civil matter whatsoever, for He was given by the Father the most absolute authority over all created things, so that all things are within His jurisdiction." Cf. St. Thomas Aquinas, *Sum. Theol.*, iii, 59, 6, ad 3 ; B. Lavaud, " la Royauté temporelle de Jésus-Christ sur l'univers," *Vie Spirituelle*, March, 1926 ; C. V. Héris, " la Royauté du Christ," *Revue des sciences philosophiques et theologiques*, July, 1926. This temporal sovereignty of Christ is exercised over nations by the intermediary of the civil, not the religious power.

[13] St. Ambrose, *Serm. contra Auxent.*

[14] " A Christian, be he king or emperor, cannot remain outside the kingdom of Christ and oppose his power to God's. The supreme commandment, ' Render to God the things that are God's,' is necessarily binding on Caesar himself, if he wants to be a Christian. He also must render to God the things that are God's, that is to say, in the first place, supreme and absolute power on earth ; because for the full understanding of the observation with regard to Caesar made by Our Lord to His enemies before the Passion, it must be completed by this more solemn observation made after His Resurrection to His disciples, the representatives of His Church : ' *All power* is given to me in heaven and *in earth* ' (Matthew xxviii. 18). Here is a formal and decisive text which cannot be interpreted with a good conscience in two ways. Those who really believe in the words of Christ will never admit a State separate from the Kingdom of God, an absolutely independent and sovereign temporal power. There is only one power on earth and that power belongs not to

Caesar but to Jesus Christ. If the observation with regard to the coin deprived Caesar of his divinity, the second observation deprives him of his *autocracy*. If he wants to rule on earth, he can no longer do so in his own right, he must constitute himself the *delegate* of Him to Whom all power on earth is given. . . .

" In revealing to humanity the Kingdom of God, which is not of this world, Christ provided all the means necessary for realising such a Kingdom in the world. Proclaiming in His pontifical prayer the perfect unity of all as the end of His work, Our Lord intended to give that work a real organic basis by founding His visible Church and appointing, to preserve her unity, a single head in the person of St. Peter. If there is any delegation of power in the Gospels, it is that. No temporal power received any sanction or promise whatever from Jesus Christ. Jesus Christ only founded the Church and He founded it on the monarchical power of Peter : ' Thou art Peter and upon this rock I will build my Church.'

" The Christian State must therefore depend on the Church founded by Christ and the Church herself depends on the chief appointed to her by Christ. . . . If the State is to be Christian, it must be subject to the Church of Christ, but if this subjection is not to be fictitious, the Church must be independent of the State, must have a centre of unity outside the State and above it, must be in truth the universal Church " (V. Soloviev, *La Russie et l'Église universelle*, pp. 74–6).

[15] Theologians (cf. C. V. Héris, *op. cit.*) tell us that the spiritual kingship of Christ has its *proximate* foundation in His capital grace, as His temporal kingship has its proximate foundation in His infused knowledge. And in the last analysis, it is, as the Encyclical *Ubi arcano* teaches, on the hypostatic union itself that this double kingship rests.

The *capital grace* of Christ is the grace He possesses as *head* of the Church, and this grace derives from Him to all whom He justifies : it is substantially identical with His personal grace : " And of His fulness we have all received " (St. John i. 16). (Cf. St. Thomas Aquinas, *Sum. Theol.*, iii, 8, 5.)

[16] Cf. C. V. Héris, *op. cit.*

[17] *Ibid.*

[18] Père Garrigou-Lagrange, " Les exigences divines de la fin dernière en matière politique," *Vie Spirituelle*, March, 1927.

[19] Bossuet, *Notes sur l'Église*, Lebarq's ed., vol. vi.

[20] " For the object of men in associating is to live a good life together, which it would be impossible for each living by himself to attain : the good life, however, is the virtuous life ; therefore, the object of human association is to live the virtuous life " (St. Thomas Aquinas, *De Regimine Principum*, i, 14).

[21] *Ibid.*

[22] " But inasmuch as, living a virtuous life, a man is ordered to an ulterior end which consists in the enjoyment of the Godhead, as we have said above, the end of the human multitude must be the same as that of the individual man. Therefore, the virtuous life is not the *ultimate* end of the associated multitude, but through a virtuous life to attain to enjoyment of the Godhead " (St. Thomas Aquinas, *De Regimine Principum*, i, 14).

[23] " Inasmuch, therefore, as the end of the good life we lead in this world is happiness in Heaven, it is the duty of the king to devise such means for the good life of the multitude as shall conduce to their attainment of happiness in Heaven : he must therefore prescribe such things as lead to happiness in Heaven and as far as possible proscribe

the opposite " (St. Thomas Aquinas, *De Regimine Principum*, i, 15). Leo XIII seems to have had this passage in mind in the Encyclical *Immortale Dei* : " It is therefore necessary that civil society, born to serve the common need, in protecting the prosperity of the State, should have such regard for the citizens as not only never to place any obstacle in the way of their pursuing and obtaining that supreme and inconvertible good they spontaneously desire, but should even afford them every opportunity it can."

[24] " For he who is concerned with the ultimate end is always found to be in a position of authority over those who are doing such things as are ordered to the ultimate end. . . . But as man does not attain the end which is enjoyment of the Godhead by human virtue, but by divine, according to the Apostle's ' *Grace of God, life everlasting* ' (Romans vi. 23), to lead to such an end will not be of human governance, but divine. Governance, therefore, of that kind pertains to that king who is not only man, but also God, *sc*., to Our Lord Jesus Christ, Who by making men the sons of God, brought them to glory in Heaven. . . . Therefore, to secure that spiritual things should be distinct from temporal things, the administration of that kingdom was entrusted not to earthly kings but to priests, and in the first place to the Highest Priest of all, the successor of Peter, the Vicar of Christ, the Roman Pontiff, to whom it behoves all Christian kings and nations to be subject as to the Lord Jesus Christ Himself.

" For even as those whose province is the care of antecedent ends ought to be subject to him whose province is the care of the ultimate end and be governed by his authority . . . so kings should be subject to priests in the law of Christ " (St. Thomas Aquinas, *De Regimine Principum*, i, 14).

[25] Innocent III, Letter *Novit ille* to the bishops of France with reference to the dispute between Philip Augustus and John Lackland. " *To judge spiritually of temporal things,*" was the expression used by Innocent IV. (Cf. Gierke's *Political Theories of the Middle Ages*, note 25 ; quoted by G. de Lagarde, *Recherches sur l'esprit politique de la Réforme*, p. 77.)

[26] Bellarmine, *De Summo Pontifice*, lib. v ; *De potestate summi Pontificis in rebus temporalibus* (against William Barclay's *De potestate Papae*, published in 1607 by William's son, John. William Barclay had died two years earlier).

[27] Suarez, *Defensio fidei catholicae et apostolicae adversus Anglicanae sectae errores*, lib. iii.

[28] " There should, therefore, exist between the two powers an ordered connection which may be not improperly compared to the union which binds the soul to the body in the case of man. . . . Whatsoever, therefore, in human affairs is in any degree sacred, whatsoever pertains to the salvation of souls or the worship of God, whether it be such of its own nature or be conceived to be such because of the cause to which it is referred, is all within the power and under the authority of the Church " (Leo XIII, Encyclical *Immortale Dei*).

" The Church," writes Pope Pius XI, in the encyclical *Ubi arcano Dei*, " was established by her Founder as a perfect society, the mistress and leader of other societies : such being the case, she will not encroach upon the authority of other societies which are each of them legitimate in their own sphere, but she will be able felicitously to complete them as grace perfects nature ; and through her such societies will be the more able to help men to attain the ultimate end which is eternal happiness and the more certain to procure for citizens happiness even on this earth . . ." And further on : " But if the Church considers it improper to meddle without reason with the government of worldly affairs and purely political matters, she is within her rights in seeking to prevent the civil power making that an excuse to oppose in any way whatsoever the superior interests which involve man's eternal salvation, to endanger or injure those interests by unjust laws or commands, to attack the divine constitution of the Church, or tread underfoot the sacred rights of God in the civil society of men."

[29] . . . " Church and State have each its own province in which each is supreme : therefore neither owes obedience to the other in the administration of its own affairs within the boundaries appointed to each " (Leo XIII, encyclical *Sapientiae Christianae*).

[30] The Bull *Unam Sanctam*, 18th November, 1302, Denz.-Bannwart, 469. Cardinal Matteo d'Aquasparta made the following declaration in the consistory held on the 24th June, 1302 : " It is also clear that nobody must cast doubt upon his competence to judge all temporal affairs *ratione peccati*. . . . For there are two jurisdictions, the spiritual and the temporal. . . . Nevertheless, the Supreme Pontiff has cognisance of all temporal affairs and can judge them *ratione peccati* " (Jean Rivière, *op. cit.*, p. 77).

[31] In his address to the consistory held on the 24th June, 1302, Boniface VIII vehemently protested against Philip the Fair's allegation " that We had ordered the king to admit that he had received his kingdom from Us. We have had forty years' experience of law and We know that there are two powers ordained by God : ought anybody, can anybody believe that such nonsense, such folly is, or ever could have been, in Our head ? We declare that in no particular do We desire to encroach upon the jurisdiction of the king and so much Our brother Porto has already said. Neither the king nor any other member

of the Faithful can deny that he is subject to us *ratione peccati.*" (Cf. Denz.-Bannwart, p. 205, note.)

[32] *Sum. Theol.*, ii—ii, 60, 6, ad 3 : " The secular power is subject to the spiritual, as the body is subject to the soul." Such an analogy had often been suggested before, more particularly by St. Gregory of Nazianzen. (Cf. Bellarmine, *De Summo Pontifice*, lib. v, cap. 6.) It was adopted by Leo XIII in the encyclical *Libertas* : " And such harmony has been not inaptly described as similar to the union between the soul and the body to the benefit of both," and in the encyclical *Immortale Dei* (*vide supra*, note 28).

[33] Bellarmine also founds his whole doctrine of the indirect power on the subordination of ends : " For this subordination [must not be understood in the sense] that one is divided from the other, but that one is subject and subordinate to the other, for the sole reason that the end of the one is subject and subordinate to the end of the other, like the subjection and subordination of the various arts to the art of governing nations which may be described as kingship " (Bellarmine, *De potestati Papae in rebus temporalibus*, cap. ii).

[34] " Infidelity by itself is not incompatible with sovereignty, for the reason that sovereignty is imported by the law of nations which is human law : the distinction between faithful and infidel, however, is of divine law which does not abrogate human law. But one committing the sin of infidelity may lose the right of sovereignty by sentence, as also occasionally for other transgressions. It is not, however, the business of the Church to punish infidelity in those who have never adopted the faith, as the Apostle says (1 Corinthians' v. 12) : ' *For what have I to do to judge them that are without ?* ' But the Church can punish by sentence the infidelity of those who have adopted the

Faith, and such are most appropriately punished by being deprived of their sovereignty over their subjects who are of the Faith : for their infidelity might turn to a great corruption of the Faith ; because, as it is said [in Proverbs vi. 12–14], '*A man that is an apostate . . . with a wicked heart he deviseth evil and at all times he soweth discord,*' scheming to lead men away from the Faith : therefore as soon as anyone is by sentence pronounced excommunicate by reason of apostasy from the Faith, his subjects are by the very fact absolved from his sovereignty and the oath of allegiance by which they were bound to him " (*Sum. Theol.*, ii–ii, 12, 2).

[35] The Church, although considering lawful authority to be derived from God and therefore to be devoutly obeyed, even when exercised by a pagan (cf. Appendix V), can also, nevertheless, by sentence of a court of law deprive an infidel prince of his authority over men whom baptism has made members of Christ. " Because infidels by reason of their infidelity deserve to lose their authority over the faithful, who are transformed into the sons of God " (St. Thomas, *Sum. Theol.*, ii–ii, 10, 10).

[36] "*Nullas minas timemus, quia de tali curia sumus quae consuevit imperare imperatoribus et regibus*" (PL, cxc, 720 D. Cf. Jean Rivière, *op. cit.*, p. 19).

[37] " It may be stated with certainty that such is the normal theory of the Middle Ages. It may have suffered distortion in times of crisis, it has ever afterwards been precisely defined and restored in its integrity " (G. de Lagarde, *op. cit.*, p. 77).

[38] In his book on the Pope (*Du Pape*, bk. ii, ch. vii) Joseph de Maistre points out that in their quarrels with kings there were never more than three objects invariably pursued by the Popes : (1) The resolute maintenance of the laws of marriage against every assault of omnipotent

licence ; (2) the preservation of the rights of the Church and the morals of the clergy ; (3) the freedom of Italy (that is to say, of the Holy See itself, which they were absolutely determined to remove from German influence).

[39] " Can anyone doubt that the priests of Christ are to be considered the fathers and masters of kings and princes and the whole body of the faithful ? " (*Epist. ad Herimannum episc.*, (1080). PL, cxlviii, 597 a).

[40] " He . . . would have us sit above kings and in judgement over kings." (Innocent III, *Epist.*, PL, ccxiv, 746.) " Whence it follows," observes M. Jean Rivière (*op. cit.*, p. 33, note 6), " that the famous clause, ' *Inasmuch as the King of France acknowledges no superior in temporal matters* ' (the Decretal *Per venerabilem*) must clearly be taken to refer to a feudal superior, not excluding the sovereign jurisdiction of the Pope."

[41] More particularly, the case of the Emperor, an elective sovereign and Emperor only through the Church, was altogether exceptional and his (indirect) temporal dependence in regard to the Church much closer than that of hereditary kings.

[42] Man being a political animal, it is so dangerous for nations, even from the point of view of the attainment of the supernatural last end, not to be at least tolerably governed in the temporal order, that the very institution of civil authority may in that sense be considered as falling within the domain of the indirect power, at all events when provision has to be made for the absence of any lawful authority and a means of escape devised from a state of political chaos as in the late Middle Ages, when bishops instituted kings. " For the truth is there to testify that the spiritual power has the right to institute the earthly power and to judge it, if it be not good " (Bull *Unam Sanctam*, Denz.-Bannwart, 469).

For a similar reason and because war of itself involves consequences injurious to the good of souls, the attempt to restrict wars or to impose the rules of Christian law on the conduct of them also normally falls within the province of the indirect power. The part played by the Church in the Middle Ages in the institution of the Truce of God is well known.

[43] Cf. on this incident, which is in the highest degree symbolical of Gallican servility in regard to the temporal power, chap. xxi of Dom Guéranger's *Institutions Liturgiques*. Austria did not suppress but was content to mutilate the legend of St. Gregory VII. (It also excised from the breviary of the Canons Regular of St. Augustine the following passage from the lesson of St. Zacharias : " *Consultus a Francis, regnum illud a Chilperico viro stupido et ignavo ad Pipinum pietate et fortitudine praestantem auctoritate Apostolica transtulit.*") In France it was only towards the middle of the nineteenth century that the right of Gregory VII to be a Saint and enjoy his lessons in the breviary in their integrity was finally acknowledged.

[44] "We do not conceal the fact that We shall shock some people by saying that We must necessarily concern ourselves with politics. But anyone forming an equitable judgement clearly sees that the Supreme Pontiff can in no wise violently separate the category of politics from the supreme control of faith and morals entrusted to him." Pius X, Consistorial Address, 9th November, 1903.

[45] Quoted by J. de Maistre, *De l'Église Gallicane*, bk. ii, chap. xiv.

[46] Jean Rivière, *op. cit.*, p. 261 (with reference to the " *Dialogue entre un clerc et un chevalier* ").

[47] The very important political part played by the Reformation in this respect should be emphasised. (Cf.

G. de Lagarde's admirable book *Recherches sur l'Esprit politique de la Réforme*.)

[48] Cf. Innocent III, Letter *Novit ille* (1204) to the bishops of France ; Boniface VIII, Bull *Ausculta fili* (5th December, 1301) and his Consistorial Address of the 24th June, 1302 ; the Bull *Unam Sanctam* (18th November, 1302) : " We are taught by the Gospel that there are two swords in this power of his [the Supreme Pontiff's], namely the spiritual and the temporal. . . . Both then are in the power of the Church, namely the spiritual and the material. The latter, however, is to be drawn in the defence of the Church, the former by the Church. . . . One sword must be under the other and the temporal authority subject to the spiritual power. . . . We must the more emphatically declare that the spiritual power takes precedence in dignity and nobility over any earthly power whatever, as things spiritual excel things temporal " (Denz.-Bannwart, 469) ; Alexander VIII's condemnation (*Inter multiplices*, 4th August, 1690) of the four articles of the Gallican clergy, the first of which declared : " . . . Kings and princes, therefore, are not subject in temporal matters to any ecclesiastical power by any ordinance of God ; neither can they be deposed directly or indirectly by the power of the keys of the Church nor their subjects dispensed from loyalty and obedience and released from their pledged oath of allegiance " (Denz.-Bannwart, 1322). Pius VI's condemnation (*Auctorem fidei*, 28th August, 1794) of the errors of the Synod of Pistoia, one of which declared that " it would be an abuse of the authority of the Church to transfer it beyond the limits of doctrine and morals and to extend it to outside matters " (Denz.-Bannwart, 1504) ; Pius IX's condemnation and inclusion in the *Syllabus* of modern errors (8th December, 1864) of the following proposition :

" The Church . . . has no direct or indirect temporal power " (Denz.-Bannwart, 1724) ; finally, the encyclicals before mentioned of Leo XIII, Pius X and Pius XI, *Immortale Dei, Pascendi, Ubi arcano Dei.*

[49] A Scholastic would say more precisely that everything in exterior and temporal things which has any reference to the *agibile, of itself* affects the subject matter in which the indirect power may have to be exercised. Things which refer to the *factibile* are only accidentally involved (to the extent that every artistic or technical operation is at the same time a human act). Politics not being a mere technique, but part of morals, exterior and temporal things within the competence of the prince and the citizen *of their very nature* come within the jurisdiction of the indirect power.

[50] " Every human action, the product of deliberate reason, considered individually, is necessarily either good or bad " (St. Thomas Aquinas, *Sum. Theol.*, i–ii, 18, 9).

[51] The *mixed* sphere properly so called is concerned with matters which, themselves bordering on the spiritual order, as, for example, public worship, religious instruction, marriage, the religious state, and being subject also to civil legislation, simultaneously, of their very nature, concern the province of the Church and civil society. The Church acts and legislates in this mixed sphere in virtue of Her *direct* power over the spiritual. (Cf. L. Choupin's *Valeur des décisions doctrinales et disciplinaires du Saint-Siège*, more particularly pp. 221–2, with reference to Proposition xxiv of the *Syllabus.*)

It may, however, be observed that the specifically temporal elements in this mixed sphere, considered apart, then fall within the jurisdiction of the indirect power ; e.g., a law enacted by the civil power in a mixed matter which, as a civil law, is a temporal thing, may be quashed and annulled by the Pope acting in virtue of his direct power (as regards the matter to which the law applies) and secondarily in virtue of his indirect power (as regards the law itself *qua* civil law).

[52] So, to quote a few examples, Benedict XIII, on the 19th December, 1729, quashed the Decree of the Parliaments of Paris and Bordeaux prohibiting the office of St. Gregory VII. " We declare," said the Pope, " the edicts, decisions, resolutions, decrees and ordinances promulgated even by supreme magistrates and every official and secular minister of any lay power whatsoever against Our said decree extending the office of St. Gregory VII . . . to be for ever null, void, invalid, of no force or effect. . . . We revoke, quash, invalidate, annul and abolish them for ever " (Dom Guéranger, *op. cit.*, p. 434). On the 30th September, 1833, Gregory XVI declared the decrees of Dom Pedro of Portugal null and void, and on the 1st February, 1836, the laws passed by the Spanish Regency in opposition to the rights of the Church ; he condemned and annulled (encyclical *Commissum Divinitus*) the *articles of Baden* which the canton of Berne had raised to the dignity of cantonal laws. So, on the 27th September, 1852, Pius IX annulled the oppressive laws passed by the Republic of New Granada (United States of Colombia) and declared " the above-mentioned decrees enacted by that government utterly null and void " (Consistorial Address *Acerbissimum*) ; on the 11th February, 1906, Pius X annulled (encyclical *Vehementer*) the French law of Separation : " In virtue of the supreme authority which God has conferred upon Us, We disapprove and condemn the law passed in France separating Church and State . . . because it is profoundly insulting to God, Whom it officially repudiates, by laying down the principle that the Republic acknowledges no form of worship,

because it is a violation of natural law, the law of nations and public fidelity to treaties, because it is opposed to the divine constitution of the Church, her essential rights and liberty . . . and We declare that it in no way affects the rights of the Church which are not to be changed by any act of violence or assault on the part of men " (Denz.-Bannwart, 1995).

In the various cases here quoted, the subject matter being mixed, the Pope intervenes in virtue of his *direct power over the spiritual*, but, also, secondarily, in virtue of his indirect power over the temporal, inasmuch, as Père de la Brière observes (cf. his article *Pouvoir pontifical dans l'ordre temporel* in the *Dictionnaire Apologétique*), as the law itself, the very act of the temporal authority, is quashed and annulled, deprived, by the authority of the Pope, of all juridical value (cf. note 51).

[53] The *non expedit* whereby, as a consequence of the despoliation of the Papal States, Pius IX and Leo XIII had forbidden Italian Catholics to take part in political elections in their country, may be recalled. The ban was subsequently raised by Pius X and Benedict XV.

[54] Père Clérissac, *Le Mystère de l'Église*. The Pope is not thereby accorded an *unlimited power over the temporal*. It is not a *direct*, but only an *indirect* power over the temporal that he is acknowledged to possess : it would be impossible for the Pope to intervene directly in military matters to teach generals lessons in strategy, or in civil affairs to prescribe to the legislature the most economical method of keeping up the highway or putting down phylloxera. . . . We have seen that the indirect power is perfectly delimited in its formal object. There must be a *ratio peccati*. But the subject matter in which such a formal object may be encountered is unlimited and it is for the Pope alone to decide in every particular case.

[55] Cf. Père Garrigou-Lagrange, *op. cit.*

[56] Were all his barons animated by the same sentiments ? Was it not they who began to show the first signs of the state of mind which was to be predominant under Philip the Fair ? What is here important is the conduct of the saintly king himself. It was always truly filial. From the fabrications of Matthew Paris to the Pragmatic Sanction (the invention, as is known, of the fifteenth century), all the allegations to the contrary of the enemies of the Holy See were pure calumnies. Cf. H. Wallon, *Saint Louis et son Temps*, and the complementary observations of Père Ch. Verdière, *Saint Louis et la monarchie chrétienne, St. Louis et l'Église de France, Saint Louis et les papes du treizième siècle* (*Études*, June, August, November and December, 1875).

[57] In 1887, the German Centre Party declined the invitation made to it by Pope Leo XIII to vote the military credits (the septennate) which Bismarck required of the Reichstag. It will be observed that this was a quite exceptional political contingency with regard to which the Pope merely expressed a wish, hoping so to facilitate the fight against the anti-religious legislation which had followed the Kulturkampf. Windhorst cannot be said to have disobeyed. The incident has nothing in common with a categorical order issued by the Church with the object of preserving the Catholic spirit and morals.

[58] Cf. Père Clérissac, *Le Mystère de l'Église*, 3rd ed., Saint-Maximin, 1925 ; preface, p. xxii.

[59] " As for infallibility, too many Catholics imagine that it is confined to the dogmatic definitions promulgated *ex cathedra* by the Pope to the universal Church and forget that besides this *extraordinary* teaching there exists an *ordinary* teaching of the Church bearing on a certain number of truths which, although they have

never been the subject of an *ex cathedra* definition by the Church, nevertheless constitute, as it were, the dogmatic patrimony of the Church, nourish the faith of its members and brook no contestation" (Père Gillet, *Revue des Jeunes*, 10th–25th March, 1927, "Les enseignements de Pie XI "). " In tracing the limits of obedience due to pastors of souls and to the Roman Pontiff especially, it must not be thought that they include only defined dogmas, the obstinate rejection of which constitutes the crime of heresy. Nor is it enough to give a sincere and unqualified assent to doctrines which, without ever having been defined by any solemn declaration of the Church, are nevertheless proposed to our belief by her ordinary and universal magistracy as of divine revelation and, since the Vatican Council, to be believed with a divine Catholic faith . . ." (Leo XIII, *Sapientiae Christianae*). The teaching of the Church is also infallible with regard to truths which, although not formally revealed, are nevertheless in close and necessary connection with revealed dogma. This point was emphasised with reference to certain moral truths in the natural order by Mgr. Ratti and his suffragans in their letter on the *Rules governing Catholic action* (1921).

[60] " Catholics are not only bound in conscience to accept and respect defined dogmas, but must also obey both doctrinal decisions proceeding from pontifical congregations and points of doctrine which, by common and constant consent, are regarded in the Church as theological truths and conclusions of such certainty that opposite opinions, even though they cannot be described as heretical, yet deserve some other theological censure " (Pius IX, *Letter to the Archbishop of Munich*, 21st December, 1863).

[61] " . . . Christians, moreover, must consider it a duty to suffer themselves to be directed, governed and controlled

by the authority of the bishops and above all by that of the Apostolic See " (Leo XIII, *Sapientiae Christianae*).

" And we cannot pass over in silence," declared Pius IX in the Encyclical *Quanta cura* (8th December, 1864), " the audacity of those who, intolerant of sound doctrine, maintain with regard to the judgements of the Holy See and its decrees, whose avowed object is the general good of the Church, her rights and discipline, that, if these are not concerned with the dogmas of faith and morals, they need not be obeyed and may be rejected without sin and without detriment to the profession of Catholicism." Anyone can perceive and immediately realise how contrary such pretensions are to the Catholic dogma of full authority divinely given by Our Lord Jesus Christ Himself to the Roman Pontiff to feed His sheep and govern the universal Church.

[62] Cf. the preceding note and on all these points Lucien Choupin's *Valeur des décisions doctrinales et disciplinaires du Saint-Siège*. 3rd ed., Paris, 1928.

[63] It is well known that besides the absolute adhesion required by infallible definitions, certain decrees of the Church require from us an interior assent of varying degree according as they bind the Church. The degree of assent is for the canonists to determine—from adhesion to an instruction of the utmost importance (such as the Encyclicals, even when they do not involve infallibility by an *ex cathedra* definition) to adhesion to a mere counsel of prudence in the actual state of our knowledge (e.g. the decisions of the Biblical Commission).

[64] St. Gregory the Great, *Homil. in Evangel.*, ii, 26, n. 6. Unjust laws, we know, are not binding in conscience ; that is to say, we are not bound to obey laws which are *unjust because of what they enjoin*, whether it be a duty imposed or allotted in such a way as is certainly contrary to the

common good, or a sin, an act intrinsically bad. (Cf. *Sum. Theol.*, i-ii, 96, 4 ; Leo XIII, Encyclical *Diuturnum illud* (29th June, 1881) : " Men have only one reason for refusing obedience, namely, if they are required to do something in flagrant opposition to natural or divine law.") With regard to an order or censure, unjust by reason of the human subject from whom it proceeds, I mean to say, *inspired by an evil motive*, the older school of theologians considered that it was nevertheless as a general rule to be obeyed, once it was decreed by a lawful superior acting within the scope of his lawful authority ; for such an act of injustice concerns the superior alone and he will be held responsible by his superior. (Cf. the testimony of Oldoricus at the Synod of Limoges in 1031. Canonists in the time of Innocent III made no distinction between the juridical validity of just and unjust censures.)   Modern opinion is that resistance to an unjust censure is permissible, but on condition that it be *absolutely clear and beyond doubt* that there be no reason for it. With this exception, the only recourse left is to appeal to a more exalted superior. And the Pope is the most exalted superior in the world. Cf. Canon 2219, § 2, of the new Code of Canon Law : *" At si dubitetur utrum poena, a superiore competente inflicta, sit justa necne, poena servanda est in utroque foro excepto casu appellationis in suspensivo."*

Clement XI condemned (Constit. dogma., *Unigenitus*, 8th September, 1713) *(inter alia)* the three following propositions of the Jansenist, Pasquier Quesnel :

" 91. Fear of unjust excommunication ought never to prevent us from doing our duty : we never leave the Church, even when we seem to be expelled from it by the wickedness of men, when we have once been attached to God, Jesus Christ and the Church itself in charity.

" 92. To suffer excommunication and an unjust

condemnation [*anathema*] in resignation rather than betray the truth is to imitate St. Paul : so far is it from rebelling against authority or destroying unity.

" 93. Jesus often heals wounds which the headlong haste of the Chief Pastors inflicts without His order : Jesus restores what their inconsidered zeal shatters " (Denz.-Bannwart, 1441–1443).

[65] " The privilege of inerrancy or infallibility guaranteed to the magistracy of the Church is not therefore to be understood in a purely negative and passive sense, such as would have God intervene only just in time to prevent a misunderstanding. The magistracy of the Church proceeds by positive judgements which imply a profound understanding, an unlimited discernment. The very formulae in which the Church sets the diamond of dogma are marvellous precious stones. But how much more precious the judgement they enclose ! There indeed is that superior form of prophecy which makes the Church a marvellous contemplative : *Manifestatio veritatis per nudam contemplationem* " (*Sum. Theol.*, ii–ii, 174, 2 ; H. Clérissac, *Le Mystère de l'Église*).

[66] The Holy Office made an astronomical mistake in condemning Galileo, but it is not impossible, even in this classic error, to perceive the divine intention referred to in the text : physico-mathematical science, a good and true thing in itself, *when perverted from its true nature and erected into a system of metaphysics, of absolute knowledge of reality (and therefore of mechanistic philosophy of which only Spinoza was later to provide the perfect form)* was bound to turn into heresy and so constitute a great danger to the human mind. The condemnation by the Church of the principal authors of this science, however regrettable in itself, gave us an obscure warning of this danger. Galileo in terms asserted the absolute character of the

mathematical knowledge of the sensible world which required three centuries to know its own nature and free itself from all heretical metaphysics. The judges in 1633 may have been blinded by human prejudice : their very mistake was far-seeing.

Galileo, moreover, would, as is well known, have been left in peace, if he had put forward the Copernican theory as a mere mathematical "hypothesis," in the sense in which the word was understood at the time. Cf. on the condemnation of Galileo, which in no way involved the infallibility of the Supreme Pontiff and was also in itself, canonically, merely a disciplinary measure, Grisar, *Galileistudien*, Regensburg, 1882 ; Jaugey, *Le procès de Galilée et la théologie*, Paris, 1888 ; Vacandard, *La Condamnation de Galilée*, in *Études de Critique et d'Histoire religieuse*, Paris, 1906 (cf. *Revue du Clergé Française* 1st and 15th October, 1904) ; Sortais, *Le procès de Galilée*, Paris, 1905 (cf. *Revue pratique d'apologétique*, 15th December, 1905) ; and above all Lucien Choupin, *Valeur des décisions doctrinales et disciplinaires du Saint-Siège*. 3rd ed., Paris, 1928.

This doctrine is not an excuse for such positive mistakes as have been made : acts of human imprudence and errors, when a government so exalted as that of spiritual things is concerned, cause incalculable damage and are of momentous importance. But I contend that, even so, there is an action of God transmitted through such human decisions, and, in spite of shortcomings which He does not desire, pursuing in a more or less obscure mystery a purpose of salvation.

[67] We so see how inadequate and defective is the comparison sometimes drawn between the obedience which is due to the Church and military obedience.

[68] Joseph de Maistre, *Du Pape*, pp. 161 and 204.

[69] " Being infallible and making a mistake, when no

right of appeal exists, are *in practice* the same thing," said Joseph de Maistre (*ibid.*, p. 212). " All Catholics are agreed . . . that when the Pontiff, either alone or in private council, issues an order in regard to some matter in doubt, he is to be obeyed by all the faithful, whether he may be right or wrong " (Bellarmine, *De Summo Pontifice*, lib. iv, c. ii).

[70] " Therefore, if the earthly power goes astray, it shall be judged by the spiritual power : and if a lesser spiritual power goes astray, by its superior : if however the supreme power goes astray, it can be judged by God alone, not by man " (Boniface VIII, Bull *Unam Sanctam*, Denz.-Bannwart, 469. Boniface then proceeds to quote 1 Corinthians ii. 15).

[71] Cf. St. Thomas Aquinas, *Sum. Theol.*, i–ii, 96, 4. The cases so contemplated by theologians (Turrecremata, Cajetan, Jacobazio, Vittoria, Bellarmine and Suarez) are theoretically possible, considered in the controversies which raged round the Pope and the Council. They are far from corresponding to any realities in history.

[72] " Of the precepts contained in the divine oracles, some refer to God, the rest to man himself and the means which lead him to eternal salvation. Now it is the province by divine right of the Church and, in the Church, of the Roman Pontiff to govern these two orders, by prescribing what ought to be believed and what ought to be done. For this reason the Supreme Pontiff must [in the order of belief] be able to judge authoritatively the content of the word of God, what doctrines are in harmony therewith and what in opposition thereto. And for the same reason [in the order of human actions], it is for him to show what is good and what is evil, what is necessary to do and to avoid doing, in order to attain salvation. Otherwise he could be neither the certain interpreter of the

word of God nor *the sure guide of human life* " (Leo XIII, Encyclical *Sapientiae Christianae*, 10th January, 1890).

[73] It will be more particularly observed that the decrees of the Index, for instance, although not infallible, have the force of universal law. " Benedict XIV, in his Brief *Quae ad Apostolicae* of the 23rd December, 1757, formally declared that the decrees of the Congregation of the Index had the force of universal law, while Leo XIII in his Constitution *Officiorum*, which lays down the law on the matter, explicitly renews this declaration " (Lucien Choupin, *op. cit.*, p. 73). The orders contained in certain consistorial addresses are also of universal validity to the extent indicated in the words used by the Pope to signify his will.

[74] Theologians teach that the disciplinary decrees of the Holy See imposing a rule of strict obligation on the universal Church can never prescribe anything contrary to moral good. ("Hence the Church cannot define whatever is honourable to be vicious or on the contrary that to be honourable which is shameful ; nor can she approve anything in her published law which is contrary to the Gospel or reason. For if the Church were to give her express approval by judgement in law to things shameful or disapprove what is honourable, this undoubted error would not only be a plague and a menace to the faithful, but also a danger to the faith, which commends every virtue and condemns all vice. The words : ' *Whatever they tell you, do*,' and ' *Whoso hears you, hears me* " suggest themselves . . . by which we are ordered to obey the laws of the Church. So that if the Church errs, Christ is the cause of our error " (Melchior Cano, *De locis theologicis*, lib. v, cap. v ; cf. Père Wernz, *Jus Decretalium*, i, n. 139). The same is true as regards a decree of the Supreme Pontiff having equivalently the force of universal law. As

Bellarmine wrote (*De potestate Summi Pontificis in rebus temporalibus*, cap. xxxi) with reference to the solemn deposition of kings, to think that an order so made could direct the commission of a sin would be to condemn the universal Church. "*Therefore anyone who says that such orders of the Vicar of Christ are not to be obeyed condemns the universal Church and ought to be described not as a canonist but really as a corrupter of canons.*"

The following further observation may be made : the theologians engaged in the case for the rehabilitation of Joan of Arc, having to give an explanation of Joan's declaration " that she left everything she had done and said to the judgement of the Church, provided that the Church did not order her to do something impossible " (that is to say, provided that the Church did not order her to deny her voices), reject the possibility of the Church—that is to say a General Council [or the Pope making a solemn declaration]—ever ordering the commission of a sinful act, even by a private individual, and even in a case in which such an act derived its sinful character not from its specific nature but from the particular circumstances determining it (such was Joan's certitude of divine faith in the truth of her voices that if she had denied them she would have sinned against faith). These theologians exclude even the hypothesis that the Church could possibly have ordered Joan to commit such a sin. Joan, they say, spoke correctly in making a supposition *per impossibile* ; a conditional proposition, as such, in no way affirms the possibility of the condition supposed. Joan no more declared that the Church could have ordered her to commit a sin than St. Paul when he wrote, "*But though . . . an angel from Heaven preach a gospel to you besides that which we have preached to you, let him be anathema*" (Galatians i. 8), affirmed that an angel from Heaven could in reality possibly lie. " If a man, even an educated man," the Chancellor Robert

205

Cybole explained in his memoir, " advanced the following conditional proposition : ' If the Council ordered me to do anything contrary to one of God's commandments, I would not do it,' I do not think that he could therefore be considered as entertaining doubtful opinions with regard to the Church and the General Council : logicians teach that a conditional proposition remains true even though the antecedent proposition is *impossible* " (Ayroles, *Jeanne d'Arc et l'Église*, vol. i, bk. iii, cap. 10 ; cf. vol. v, bk. iv, cap. 4). " Nor does she admit the possibility of any conflict between Our Lord and the Church : ' *They are all one*,' she says. . . . In Joan's opinion it is such an elementary truth that no difficulty ought to arise : ' *Why do you see any difficulty in their being all one* ? ' " (*ibid.*, vol. v, bk. iii, cap. 14, p. 281). " She knew very well," concludes Père Ayroles, " that the true Church could not condemn her, but she felt, or the divine Spirit which made her speak knew, that she was in the presence of people who usurped the honour of being the Church " (*ibid.*, p. 382). Nothing, therefore, could be more outrageous to the Church than to compare one of her authentic deeds to the action of men who diabolically aped the Church and refused Joan the right of appeal to the Pope in Rome on the pretext that he was too far away. The regalian and schismatical tendencies of these Churchmen revealed themselves finally at the Council of Bâle.

[75] " Now, therefore, if we are bound by the law of nature to love and cherish above all things the State in which we have been born and have first seen the light to such an extent that the good citizen should have no hesitation in even laying down his life for his country, it is the duty of Christians to a far greater extent constantly to feel such sentiments with regard to the Church. For the Church is the holy State of the living God, born of God

Himself and founded by Him : she sojourns in the world but her call is to mankind whom she instructs and leads to eternal happiness in Heaven. We should therefore feel a passionate love for our country, the source of our mortal life : but love of the Church must take first place, for to the Church we are indebted for the everlasting life of the soul " (Leo XIII, Encyclical *Sapientiae Christianae*, 10th January, 1890).

[76] Cf. Pius IX, Encyclical *Cum Catholica Ecclesia*, 26th March, 1860 ; *Syllabus*, 8th December, 1864, props. 75 and 76 ; Leo XIII, Encyclical *Inscrutabili Dei Consilio*, 21st April, 1878 ; Encyclical *Etsi Nos*, 13th February, 1882 ; Letter to Cardinal Rampolla, 15th June, 1887 ; Pius X, Encyclical *E Supremi Apostolatus*, 4th October, 1903 ; Benedict XV, Encyclical *Ad Beatissimi*, 1st November, 1914 ; Encyclical *Pacem Dei*, 23rd May, 1920 ; Pius XI, Encyclical *Ubi arcano Dei*, 23rd December, 1922.

[77] With reference to the Action Française Catholics, " It is of supreme importance," I wrote at the time (19th September, 1926), " both for them and for the future of France to bear in mind the *supernatural* quality which should inform Christian obedience. I would here recall the general doctrine which I merely echoed elsewhere.[1] The Church is simultaneously human and divine. Leave her infallible decisions out of account. Even though, in another sphere, the precept or counsel imparted by the Church were to appear to the individual mind of any one of us inopportune or ill-founded, even though we had the most excellent reasons to complain of the series of events determining it in the human order, such a series of subordinate causes is in the circumstances entirely of secondary importance ; there is always a divine message, a certain

[1] In the Preface to Père Clérissac's book *Le Mystère de l'Église*, 3rd ed., Saint-Maximin, 1925.

intention of the spirit of God transmitted through the intermediary of such human events which the spirit of faith can always discover. 'Père Clérissac declared that, even without the intervention of an express injunction, it was always possible to distinguish the pure spiritual line in accordance with which the order inspired from above became binding on the virtue of obedience. He added that so respectful a deference to authority required the nicest discernment according to the kinds and degrees of subordination and injunction ; for it related to a living and free docility of the practical judgement, not to a servile and mechanical compliance.' Such a doctrine is of absolutely capital importance. It is the great error of Catholics that they forget it only too often.

" What is important to avoid is greater evils, and in such a case the greatest misfortune for a son of the Church would not be disobedience (there could be no question of that), but an obedience controlled and regulated by motives and reasons of the human and natural order, not by the spirit of faith : a semi-obedience unworthy of a Christian " (*Une Opinion*, etc., pp. 58–9 and 62–3).

[78] Père Clérissac, *Le Mystère de l'Église.*

[79] What is described as the *spirit of faith* implies not only the theological virtue of faith, but the gift of the Holy Ghost which is called the gift of understanding and which makes us give our assent to the invisible truth of divine things without risk of error or scandal, in spite of the obstacles which may arise from appearances. (Cf. John of St. Thomas, *Curs. Theol.*, vi, *De Donis.* A French translation of this treatise, *Les Dons du Saint-Esprit*, by Mme Jacques Maritain, with a preface by Père Garrigou-Lagrange, has been published, January, 1930.)

[80] Pius X, speech to the priests of *l'Union Apostolique* (quoted from Henri Brun's " *La Société Chrétienne*," p. 312).

It is important to observe with the distinguished and learned Fr. Faber that the Pope in the Christian economy is entitled not only to respect and filial love but also to devotion in the proper sense of the term : " Devotion to the Pope is an essential part of all Christian piety. It is not a matter which stands apart from the spiritual life. . . . It is a doctrine and a devotion. It is an integral part of Our Blessed Lord's own plan. He is in the Pope in a still higher way than He is in the poor or in children. What is done to the Pope, for him or against him, is done to Jesus Himself. All that is kingly, all that is priestly, in Our dearest Lord, is gathered up in the person of His Vicar, to receive our homage and veneration. A man might as well try to be a good Christian without devotion to Our Lady as without devotion to the Pope, and for the same reason in both cases. Both His Mother and His Vicar are parts of Our Lord's Gospel." Cf. *Devotion to the Pope* (a tract published in 1860), *being the substance of a sermon preached in the church of the London Oratory on the occasion of the solemn Exposition of the Blessed Sacrament for the intention of the Pope on the first day of the New Year*, 1860. Cf. also *Life of Father Faber*, by J. E. Bowden, priest of the Oratory, London, 1869, at pp. 368–9.

[81] Cf. more especially Pius XI's letter to Cardinal Andrieu of the 5th September, 1926 : " Your Eminence is therefore well advised to leave out of account purely political questions, such as, for example, the form of government. In that regard the Church allows everyone a proper freedom " ; and the consistorial address of the 20th December, 1926 : " Let everyone retain the right and proper freedom to prefer whatever form of government he likes, provided it be not at variance with the order of things established by God."

[82] Père Garrigou-Lagrange, *op. cit.*

[83] I referred to such dangers in my pamphlet in the following terms : " From the point of view of political science, there is also a danger of confining oneself entirely to empiricism as a sufficient doctrine and rejecting higher syntheses which alone can lead to science in the proper sense of the term. The error into which there is then a risk of falling is the error of political ' naturalism.'

" From the religious point of view, there is a danger of considering the Church in the supernumerary benefits she dispenses as being the strongest bulwark of the social good rather than in her end and function and essential dignity which are to provide mankind with supernatural truth and the means to eternal salvation, and in virtue of which she acquires the right to intervene in temporal matters. An apologetic which would lay most stress upon the human and social aspect, such an apologetic as Brunetière and Paul Bourget have developed, is certainly legitimate but utterly inadequate. And, if it is true, and we have the direct testimony of Leo XIII for it, that one indication of the divine mission of the Church is to be found in the fact that the Church alone offers a supreme and effective guarantee for the upright temporal life of nations, it is also true that the supernatural life here introduced by the Church, the kingdom of Heaven in our midst, is of such a transcendent nature, so peculiarly divine, that Catholicism, as Paul Claudel recently observed with such force,[1] will never be able to find itself really *at home* among the kingdoms of the earth and that the order of charity will always infinitely transcend the best established human order. The State, as such, has duties to God, and Church and State must, because of such duties and for the good of souls, be united. Such is the law, what justice requires, and that is what is of most importance. In fact, however, and with a few saintly exceptions, whom she

[1] In his preface to Jacques Rivière's book, *A la trace de Dieu.*

proposes for our admiration, the Church has almost suffered as much at the hands of Christian kings in defence of her independence as from anti-Christian governments in defence of her existence. Christ is King in every sense of the word, King of nations as of Heaven, but on being offered the temporal sovereignty which is His by right, He refused to exercise it, thereby indicating to us a great mystery of the historic life of His mystical Body. If the truths above mentioned concerning the necessary political conditions of an upright human life are to be preserved intact, a certain pessimism regarding the course of human events and politics in the first place befits the Christian, who has no dwelling place here below, a pessimism inclining him to place but little reliance on the establishment of political conditions wholly and permanently good, and to hope but little from the best of governments : *nolite confidere in principibus.* But what he must hate *in his capacity as citizen* [1] and strive to overthrow, unless some greater evil must befall the State, is a political sovereignty not accidentally, but essentially in law and principle opposed to Christ " (*Une Opinion*, etc., pp. 47–51).

[84] " And so all these poor children allowed themselves to be carried away by fables, fables about documents forged and burned, fables about anti-patriotic, anti-French conspiracies, fables about some dream of restoring

[1] It is the very good (spiritual and material) of the human State, considered both in the order of its peculiar (temporal) life and as destined to prepare for the attainment of the supernatural life of souls (eternal life), which makes the temporal and political struggle against persecution unavoidable. The Christians of the early centuries did not attempt to overthrow the persecuting Empire because, being absolutely powerless to establish a Christian State, they had the good fortune to be obliged to devote their minds only to eternal life and supernatural interests (considered solely in themselves and not in the temporal preparations they normally require). Their rebellion, even supposing it could have been successful, would have succeeded simply in jeopardising the existence of the State. They were left with martyrdom and martyrdom is not the worst solution.

the Holy Roman Empire : fables so absurd that in the face of them there was nothing to be done but repeat the prayer of good St. Philip Neri that God would keep His holy hand upon his head " (Pope Pius XI, Address to the Superiors and Pupils of the French Seminary, 25th March, 1927). " . . . They say again that We are working in a party spirit for the restoration of an Empire, or else that, carried away by Our devotion to one nation more than another, We are exceeding the limits of Our authority and ordering what is contrary to patriotism. Such allegations are supremely insulting to Us, and are not merely in contradiction with Our repeated formal declarations and the most manifest truth : they border on mania. To these insubordinate children We have no hesitation in addressing the admonition of the Apostle : ' *But to me it is a very small thing to be judged by you or by man's day ; but neither do I judge my own self . . . but he that judgeth me is the Lord* ' " (Pius XI, consistorial address of the 20th June, 1927).

[85] " The Pope did that as he does everything within the sphere of his apostolic ministry, with the sole object of fulfilling his duty which is to procure the glory of God and the salvation of souls, to prevent evil and to procure good outside and above all political parties ; that is the great rule which he never ceases to recall to everyone and which he is the first to follow " (Address of Pius XI to the French pilgrims, 25th September, 1926). " Although We consider it superfluous, nevertheless We add ' out of the fullness of the heart,' as they say, that Our past and present observations have not been and are not inspired by prejudice or party zeal or human considerations or imperfect inappreciation of, or insufficient regard for, the benefits which Church or State has derived from certain men or associations of men or political schools, but simply

and solely out of respect to, and in the consciousness of, an obligation imposed by Our office to protect the honour of the divine King, the salvation of souls, the good of religion and the future prosperity of Catholic France itself" (Pius XI, consistorial address of the 20th December, 1926).

[86] Cf. *Mercure de France*, 1st April, 1927.

[87] The same observations may be made with reference to the condemnation of *l'Avenir* by Gregory XVI. Cf. H. A. Noble, *Lacordaire et la condamnation de " l'Avenir."* Ed. *Revue des Jeunes.* Lacordaire being accused by Baron d'Eckstein " of having abandoned his father," " beaten his nurse," " trodden the weak and the oppressed under foot," retorted as follows : " My nurse in the spiritual order was the Church : my father was Jesus Christ. I preferred them to a man, because a Christian never pledges himself but saving the allegiance he owes them. I had solemnly promised, when we set out for Rome, to listen with the docility of a child to the slightest word of the Vicar of Christ. That word was spoken : I never hesitated for a moment ; I bowed before it, logical with myself, faithful to that respect for the Holy See so loudly proclaimed in the school which I had embraced. . . . I am, however, accused of kicking a man on the ground. No ; courage ever consisted in defending the weak, the oppressed and the victims of circumstance ; in the present case it is truth which is weak : the oppressed is the Church to whom nobody gives a thought and upon whom they seek to impose the ideas of a man under penalty of being considered ungrateful and persecuting ; the victims are all those young men who are compromised by a solidarity the extent of which it was impossible to foresee." [1]

" Your error, my dear friend," he wrote again to Montalembert,[2] " lay in following a man instead of author-

---

[1] *Univers religieux*, 28th June, 1834.   [2] 2nd December, 1833.

ity and in believing in talent more than in the Holy Ghost. . . . Do you know what will happen to-morrow? Are you aware of the fate of Europe? Are you sure that this liberalism you are so fond of will not beget the most formidable kind of slavery which ever oppressed the human race? Are you quite certain that it will not re-establish the slavery of antiquity, that your children will not groan under the godless whip of the all-conquering republican? You may be blaspheming what is preserving your children from shame and misery. In an ephemeral certainty of conviction, which you may regret in ten years' time, you are rebelling against the highest authority there is in the world, against the vessel of the Holy Ghost! You are relying upon trifling distinctions between the spiritual and the temporal to escape the consequences of your faith!"

[88] Père Garrigou-Lagrange, *op. cit.*

[89] "Man is subject both in relation to natural happiness, either individual or political, and in relation to supernatural happiness." Cajetan in *Sum. Theol.*, i–ii, 92, 1; cf. Appendix V, *ante, On Liberalism.*

[90] Without drawing any comparison with the nationalism of the Action Française, it may be observed that a certain form of nationalism, Polish " radical nationalism," was condemned by Pius X in 1905 on account of the violent demonstrations it provoked (Pius X, *Poloniae Populum,* 3rd December, 1905).

[91] St. Thomas considers the *regimen mixtum* to be the best system (*Sum. Theol.*, i–ii, 95, 4). Cf. Marcel Demongeot, *La Théorie du Régime mixte chez Saint Thomas d'Aquin,* a thesis maintained before the Faculty of Law of the University of Paris, 1927, and since published under the title of *Le meilleur régime politique selon St. Thomas,* Paris, Blot, 1928.

[92] This is the title of a pamphlet written in defence of Richelieu's policy at the Cardinal's request by Jérémie Ferrier, a former Calvinist professor of theology who became converted and was "nominally a Catholic but more preoccupied with the claims of the State than the rights of the Church" : *Le Catholique d'Estat, ou Discours politique des alliances du Roy très-chrestien contre les calomnies des ennemis de son Estat*. The name which the "good Catholics" at the Roman Curia and in France used to stigmatise the Cardinal thus became a rallying word. Cf. H. Fouqueray's *Histoire de la Compagnie de Jésus en France des origines à la suppression*, vol. iv, ch. i.

[93] Père Clérissac, *La Messagère de la politique divine*, No 2 of *Chroniques* in the Roseau d'Or, 1926.

[94] Such calumnies are long lived. Dante, as is well known, has no tenderness for the memory of Boniface VIII; but Dante is not a particularly reliable source of information in matters of ecclesiastical history. With regard to the charges he makes against the Popes, cf. Bellarmine, *De Summo Pontifice*, Appendix (in reply to the *Aviso piacevole dato alla bella Italia da un nobile giovane Francese*). "The animadversions of Dante, a member of the Ghibelline faction, against the Popes and the clergy ought rightly to be regarded as suspect, for Dante seems to have applied his mind to writing rather out of hatred for his enemies than for love of truth" (cap. 14).

[95] The formula of the liberal error later condemned by the Church and then invoked by a king who dreamed of becoming supreme over the Church and "revived in the heyday of Christendom the tradition of the Byzantine Empire" (Jean Rivière, *op. cit.*, p. 121).

[96] "A long time already before war, through the fault of individuals and nations, set Europe ablaze, the principal cause of so many misfortunes was developing

its action : this cause would have been removed and destroyed by the very fear of war, if the significance of those appalling events had been generally understood. Who is there who does not know the words of Scripture . . . *they that have forsaken the Lord shall be consumed* (Isaias, i. 28). The momentous words of Christ, the Redeemer and Master of men, are equally familiar : . . . *without me you can do nothing* (John xv. 5), and again . . . *he that gathereth not with me, scattereth* (Luke xi. 23).

" These divine judgements have been realised at all times ; now they are being verified more than ever before the eyes of all. It is because they have pitiably strayed far from God and Jesus Christ that men have fallen from their former prosperity and now welter in this morass of troubles ; and for the same reason all their attempts to repair the loss and preserve what remains of so many ruins are rendered for the most part vain and fruitless. God and Jesus Christ being therefore excluded from law and government, authority seeks its source no longer in God, but in man ; the first consequence is that laws are deprived of the real substantial guarantees and the supreme principles of justice which even pagan philosophers, such as Cicero, conceived to be solely situate and enclosed within the external law of God ; the very foundations of authority are thereby sapped and the primary reason justifying in one case the right to command and in the other the duty to obey is abolished. . . .

" It must be observed that the doctrine and the rules laid down by Christ with regard to the dignity of human personality, the purity of morals, the duty of obedience, the organisation by God of the human society, the sacrament of marriage and the sanctity attaching to the Christian family, His teaching and all the truths He came to bring from Heaven to earth, have been entrusted by Christ to the exclusive custody of His Church. . . .

" The Church alone having, by reason of the truth and power of Christ invested in her, the task of forming souls to virtue, can alone at the present day restore the true peace of Christ and guarantee it for the future by removing the fresh danger of war to which we have referred. The Church alone, by her mission and the order of God, teaches that the eternal law of God ought to serve for rule and measure to every human activity, public or private, individual or social " (Pius XI, encyclical *Ubi arcano Dei*, 23rd December, 1922).

[97] Dom Guéranger, *Institutions Liturgiques.*

[98] Père Garrigou-Lagrange, *op. cit.*

[99] St. Thomas Aquinas, *Sum. Theol.*, ii–ii, 26, 7 and 8. If it leaves this order, it becomes corrupted. The 64th proposition of the *Syllabus* condemned by Pius IX may be recalled : " The violation of an oath however sacred and every criminal and shameful action opposed to the eternal law are not only not reprehensible, but absolutely lawful and worthy of the highest praise, when inspired by love of country " (Denz.-Bannwart, 1746). " Love of country and the race to which we belong is certainly a powerful incentive," wrote Pius XI, " to excite manifold virtues and noble exploits, provided it be governed by the Christian law ; but it becomes a source of innumerable injustices and disorders when it transgresses the bounds of justice and law and proceeds to extravagances in an unbridled nationalism. Those who allow themselves to be carried away by it necessarily end by losing sight of the fact that all nations, being members of the great single human family, are bound together in fraternal relations and that other nations also are entitled to live and work for their prosperity ; they also forget that it is neither permissible nor useful to separate interest and morality. *Justice exalteth a nation : but sin maketh nations miserable*

(Proverbs xiv. 34). That a family, a city, a State, should secure its own advantage by injuring others, men may consider a clever and glorious feat ; but such grandeur is unstable and should dread a catastrophe, as St. Augustine wisely warns us : *Happiness, fragile as glass, for which a man should tremble and be afraid lest it suddenly break.*" *De Civ. Dei*, iv, c. iii. (encyclical *Ubi arcano Dei*).

[100] I may be permitted to refer to some words of mine in a recent essay on *La Politique de Pascal* : " Real not feigned justice is the ' mystic foundation ' of the authority of law as of peace in the state. If this first order, which consolidates human affairs by the divine stabilities of the universe, is shattered, the strongest empirical defences of the social order will be of little avail. How infinitely more enlightened, more genuinely realist was the statecraft of St. Catharine of Siena than Pascal's, when she exclaimed to the leaders of the people : *Sacred justice is the strongest bulwark of preservation.* Pascal did not perceive that it was an outrage on the author of all being to banish justice and therefore the order of eternal wisdom from the principle of human laws and the State. He did not perceive that, the State being intended for the fulfilment of the ends of human nature in accordance with that eternal order, it was a pure and simple contradiction in terms to pretend to ensure the good of the State on a basis of injustice " (*Réflexions sur l'intelligence*, ch. v, Paris, 1924). This is as applicable to the interior government of the State as to its relations with other States.

To maintain relations of justice between nations, the Church has always desired the existence of a community of nations (the political organisation of Christendom) which, without injury to the rights of the various States or societies capable of being self-sufficient (" perfect societies "), should play a controlling and pacificatory part among them. "Modern states have attained such a degree of interdependence," M. Le Fur wrote recently (*Lettres*, 1st March, 1927), "that life in society is almost as much a necessity for them as for individuals. . . . It becomes increasingly apparent that an organised community of nations (with a Court of international justice which is the concrete translation of the spirit of international justice) is the only means of saving the world from the ruins which an unbridled nationalism fatally brings in its train." But such an *international* temporal organism (of positive, not natural, law, as some people are inclined to think) is not only incapable of taking the place of the *supranational* spiritual unity of the Church of Christ, but will also always run the risk of being more dangerous than beneficent, if it does not admit the principles of Christian law and the genuine subordination of the temporal to the spiritual.

"Moreover there is no human institution capable of imposing on all nations a sort of code of common laws adapted to our times, as was the case in the Middle Ages for that true league of nations which the community of Christian nations was. In that Christendom justice was, no doubt, only too often violated in fact : but the sanctity of justice, at all events, remained intact in principle as an infallible rule to which the nations themselves were answerable.

"There is, however, a divine institution which can preserve the sacred character of the law of nations, an institution which affects all nations and is superior to all nations, invested with a supreme authority, with the religious prestige of a supreme and perfect magistracy : that institution is the Church of Christ. She alone seems to be capable of coping with such an arduous task through the mandate she has received from God, by her very nature and constitution and, not least, by that incomparable secular majesty which the storms of war, so far from destroying, have merely strengthened to a marvellous degree " (Pius XI, encyclical *Ubi arcano Dei*, 23rd December, 1922).

[101] " Exclusivism and universality are the characteristics of the Church of the Old Testament (and they will be continued, in a completed sense, to the Church of the New).

" Exclusivism in the present : universality in the future.

" Exclusivism on the part of God, Who encloses in Israel His manifestations and promises, Who cloisters His people and seals its flesh with the seal of His union. Exclusivism on the part of Israel, which appropriates to itself a God Whose transcendence it yet perfectly realises, and considers all nations with a nobler and loftier contempt than that which the Greeks and Romans had for the Barbarians.

" Universality, most intelligent and most human, if one may say so, on the part of God as on the part of Israel ; for the Decalogue appeals not to a local conscience, but to the conscience of all mankind ; and the Jerusalem of Messianic times is the vision of a country which is chiefly spiritual, the country of souls. The prophets speak and strive with the sole object of securing this predominance of the kingdom of God which is in men's hearts to begin with and embraces all nations.

" Such exclusivism and universality will in time become Catholic Unity, which is forever the absolute characteristic of the Work of the Lord Jesus " (Père H. Clérissac, *Le Mystère de l'Église*).

[102] Bull *Unam Sanctam*. " Furthermore We declare, affirm, define and proclaim that submission to the Roman Pontiff is absolutely of the necessity of salvation for every human creature " (Denz.-Bannwart, 469). The formula here adopted by Boniface VIII was already to be found

in St. Thomas Aquinas, *Contra errores Graecorum*, ii, 27. "For it is shown that submission to the Roman Pontiff is of the necessity of salvation." Souls born in schism or not incorporated within the Church by means of the sacraments but in a state of grace, nevertheless, by reason of their good faith, belong virtually and invisibly (*voto*) to the visible Church and are therefore under the spiritual jurisdiction of the Roman Pontiff.

[103] *Chroniques* of the Roseau d'Or series, No. 1, 1925.

[104] A remarkable application of the doctrine of the indirect power of the Sovereign Pontiff over temporal things may be found, let it be observed in passing, in the ideas of Las Casas on the right of colonisation. [On Las Casas cf. Marcel Brion's *Bartolomé de Las Casas, Père des Indiens*, No. 28 of the Roseau d'Or series, Paris, 1928.]

[105] It would be altogether unjust not to associate the names of other Spanish missionaries with the great name of Bartolomé de Las Casas. In this connection, in their Pastoral Letter of the 12th December, 1926, on the persecution then raging in Mexico, the U.S. Bishops, after observing that the ancient pagan civilisation of Mexico had disappeared long before the missionaries set foot in the New Continent, continue as follows : " Murder and cannibalism had attained the dignity of religious rites. The ancient civilisation, long since extinct, had left part of its history behind in legend and ruin. As for the new civilisation introduced by the Spanish missionaries, its monuments are still standing, its achievements are inscribed in historical records. Now the laws governing the Indians have been considered as the most just code ever devised for the protection of aborigines (Lummis, *Awakening of a Nation*, Introduction). A comparison of the situation of the Mexican Indian in the early nineteenth century with that of his Northern brother shows at once that the work

of the Catholic missionary was both beautiful and good. The results of his work are seen to continue to this day. The praise and honour which have been heaped on Juarez, for example, are not undeserved, at all events so far as his intelligence and ability are concerned. But such praise and honour are properly attributable to the Church which he persecuted, for it was she who made such as Juarez possible. An Indian such as Juarez would be a prodigy in the United States. He was not so in Mexico, where great men have sprung and continue to spring from the native population.

"The Church had laid the foundations before her action was thwarted and calumniated. Miguel de Cabrera was the greatest painter in Mexico ; he was an Indian. In the same sphere, Panduro and Velasquez are still reckoned among Indian glories. Altamirano, the great orator, novelist, poet and journalist, was also an Indian. Juan Esteban, a simple lay brother of the Society of Jesus, was a teacher of such eminence that Spanish families made their children cross the Ocean to enjoy the original methods and effective instruction of that Indian. Amongst orators, an Indian bishop, Nicholas del Puerto, occupies a distinguished place. In the sphere of high philosophy, the world has produced few men like the Archbishop Munguia de Michoacao. Francisco Pascual Garcia was a great jurist, Ignacio Ramirez a distinguished journalist, Rodriguez Gavan a distinguished poet and at the same time a journalist ; Bartolomé de Alba was a sound and convincing preacher ; Diego Adriano and Agustin de la Fuente were master printers ; Adriano de Tlaltelolco, an accomplished Latinist. They were all Indians. The historians Ixtlilxochitl and Valeriano were also Indians. Rincon was the author of the best grammar of the Aztec language. He, like De Alba, was descended from the kings of Texcoco. The bibliography of works written by Mexicans before the first revolution fills many stout volumes ; the Indians take up considerable room. To whom is the honour due ? To that Church which the Mexican government accuses before the world of having contributed nothing to its country" (*Revue Catholique des Idées et des Faits*, 18th March, 1927 ; *Documentation Catholique*, 26th March, 1927).

The sufferings heroically borne by the Church in Mexico in our day during the last persecution recall the virtues of her founders. In his *Praxis theologiae mysticae*, Fr. Michel Godinez, himself an admirable missionary and famous spiritual director, testifies to their labours and their sanctity and to the fruitful nature of the contemplation which sustained them. " I was acquainted with some of those missionaries to whom God had communicated the highest degrees of infused contemplation. One I knew well remained rapt in ecstasy for three days and nights on end ; others, whom I also knew, enjoyed the vision of celestial things in the highest contemplation for four or six consecutive hours. There is the source of abundant harvests. . . ."

[106] This war ought to be more exactly described as a *war of hucksters*. With reference to the waves of xenophobia which have passed over China, " their origin may be ascribed," Mgr. Beaupin recently wrote, " to the very circumstances which compelled China about 1840 to open her frontiers to foreign invasion. Until that date, only the Russians had succeeded, in 1689, in signing a treaty with China authorising merchants in the possession of passports to trade freely throughout the Empire. A century and a half later English cannon compelled the government of Peking to receive English ships and dealers in some of their harbours. This was what is improperly described as the Opium War, because the import of

that commodity into China was not the sole cause of the conflict" (*Documentation Cath.*, 21st May, 1927). That opium was not the sole cause of the war is of small importance : one of its objects was to compel China to open her doors to trading in that commodity ; but what is of very great importance, no law, human or divine, sanctions the making of war on a people to compel them to import and export and not to withdraw their natural resources from the universal circulation of riches. War so waged in the name of the divine Rights of Trade can only be considered as a sin and a disgrace.

" Two agents of the East India Company," writes M. Huc in his famous Memoirs, " were the first who, in the beginning of the eighteenth century, conceived the deplorable thought of sending to China the opium of Bengal. Colonel Watson and Vice-President Wheeler are the persons to whom the Chinese are indebted for this new system of poisoning. History has preserved the name of Parmentier ; why should it not also those of these two men ? Whoever has done either great good or great harm to mankind ought to be remembered, to excite either gratitude or indignation.

" At present, China purchases annually of the English opium of the amount of seven millions sterling : the traffic is contraband, but is carried on along the whole coast of the Empire and especially in the neighbourhood of the five ports which have been opened to Europeans. Large fine vessels, armed like ships of war, serve as depots to the English merchants, and the trade is protected not only by the English government, but also by the mandarins of the Celestial Empire. The law which forbids the smoking of opium under pain of death, has indeed never been repealed, but every one smokes away quite at his ease notwithstanding. Pipes, lamps, and all the apparatus for smoking opium are sold publicly in every town, and the mandarins themselves are the first to violate the law and give this bad example to the people, even in the courts of justice. During the whole of our long journey through China, we met but with one tribunal where opium was not smoked openly and with impunity " (*The Chinese Empire, A Sequel to Recollections of a Journey through Tartary and Thibet*, by M. Huc, formerly missionary apostolic in China, Longmans, etc., London, 1860, pp. 18–19).

[107] Pius XI, as is known, himself consecrated six Chinese bishops on the 28th October, 1926 (cf. the article by Léopold Levaux on *la Chine et les Missions*, in *Chroniques* of the Roseau d'Or series, No. 2).

[108] *Bulletin des Missions*, published by the Benedictines of Saint-André, January–February, 1927.

[109] *Chroniques* of the Roseau d'Or series, No. 1, 1925.

[110] C. H., *Abrégé de toute la doctrine mystique de Saint Jean de la Croix*, preface (Saint-Maximin, 1925).

[111] Cf. the *Apostolic Constitution of Pope Pius XI approving the statutes of the Carthusian Order revised in accordance with the provisions of the Code of Canon Law*, 8th July, 1924. The following passage is an extract from that document : " Those who profess to lead a life of solitude far from the worries and the follies of the world—not only with the object of applying the whole force of their minds to the contemplation of the divine mysteries and eternal truths and making unceasing supplication to God for the daily increasing expansion and extension of His kingdom, but also to efface and do penance for their sins and the sins also of their neighbours by mortifications of the spirit and the body voluntarily determined and prescribed by their Rule, have, certainly, like Mary of Bethania, chosen the better part. If the Lord grants such a vocation, no more perfect state or condition of life can be proposed to the choice and

ambition of men. . . ." Then, after recalling the life of the early anchorites and their gathering together, in the train of Anthony, in rude huts in the desert, whence the institution of communal life imperceptibly arose : " It is astonishing," the pontifical document continues, " to see what services were rendered to Christian society by such an institution which was entirely based upon the exclusive application of the monks to the contemplation of the heavenly realities, each living in the secrecy of his cell, free and independent of every exterior duty. It was impossible for the clergy and the people of the time not to consider such men as a magnificent example, from which they might derive great profit, who, drawn by the love of Christ to what was most perfect and austere, reproduced the interior hidden life which the Lord Himself had led in the house at Nazareth and so completed, like victims consecrated to God, whatever was lacking in the sufferings of the Passion. Nevertheless, this absolutely perfect institution of the contemplative life lost in course of time some of its primitive ardour and strength : for, although the monks refrained from the direction of souls and other exterior duties, gradually, little by little, they came to combine the works of the active life with meditation and the contemplation of divine things. . . . Now God, in His goodness, Who never ceases to supply the needs and tend the welfare of His Church, then raised up Bruno, a man of eminent sanctity, to restore to the contemplative life the lustre of its primitive sanctity. With that object Bruno founded the Carthusian Order" (*Acta*, 15th October, 1924).

The teaching contained in this very important document is not opposed to the classical doctrine of St. Thomas on the superiority pure and simple of the mixed life. But the latter, in which action ought to overflow entirely from the superabundance of contemplation, really implies in its concept perfection itself, so that the state most fully answering it is the episcopal state or perfection possessed. The religious state is the state not of *acquired* perfection but of perfection *to be acquired* : if the divers forms of religious life are to be judged according to their object considered in itself, it must be admitted with St. Thomas that that is the most perfect which, implying works *per se* proceeding from contemplation, approximates most to the episcopal state or acquired perfection, but if they are to be judged according to the conditions in which they put the subject to progress to perfection, it cannot be denied that the greatest progress towards perfection is made in the purely contemplative forms of religious life, in which the redemption of souls is achieved only through penance and love, so that from this point of view, " no more perfect state or condition of life can be proposed to the choice and ambition of men."

The insistence with which Pius XI dwells in the encyclical *Rerum Ecclesiae* on the desirability of establishing contemplative communities in missionary countries may also from this same point of view be noted.

[112] Vol. ii, p. 314, of the critical edition (French translation by H. Hoornaert, Paris, 1922-3).

[113] *Une Opinion*, etc., p. 39.

[114] St. John of the Cross, *Spiritual Canticle*, str. 29 ; *Spiritual Maxims*.